ETHICS IN CITY HALL

DISCUSSION AND ANALYSIS *for* PUBLIC ADMINISTRATION

WILLIAM N. THOMPSON, PhD
PROFESSOR OF PUBLIC ADMINISTRATION
UNIVERSITY OF NEVADA–LAS VEGAS
LAS VEGAS, NEVADA

JAMES E. LEIDLEIN, MPA
CITY MANAGER
HARPER WOODS, MICHIGAN
ADJUNCT FACULTY–POLITICAL SCIENCE
WAYNE STATE UNIVERSITY
DETROIT, MICHIGAN

JONES AND BARTLETT PUBLISHERS
Sudbury, Massachusetts
BOSTON   TORONTO   LONDON   SINGAPORE

World Headquarters

Jones and Bartlett Publishers
40 Tall Pine Drive
Sudbury, MA 01776
978-443-5000
info@jbpub.com
www.jbpub.com

Jones and Bartlett Publishers
Canada
6339 Ormindale Way
Mississauga, Ontario L5V 1J2
Canada

Jones and Bartlett Publishers
International
Barb House, Barb Mews
London W6 7PA
United Kingdom

Jones and Bartlett's books and products are available through most bookstores and online booksellers. To contact Jones and Bartlett Publishers directly, call 800-832-0034, fax 978-443-8000, or visit our website www.jbpub.com.

Substantial discounts on bulk quantities of Jones and Bartlett's publications are available to corporations, professional associations, and other qualified organizations. For details and specific discount information, contact the special sales department at Jones and Bartlett via the above contact information or send an email to specialsales@jbpub.com.

This publication is designed to provide accurate and authoritative information in regard to the Subject Matter covered. It is sold with the understanding that the publisher is not engaged in rendering legal, accounting, or other professional service. If legal advice or other expert assistance is required, the service of a competent professional person should be sought.

Production Credits
Acquisitions Editor: Jeremy Spiegel
Editorial Assistant: Maro Asadoorian
Production Director: Amy Rose
Senior Production Editor: Renée Sekerak
Production Assistant: Julia Waugaman
Associate Marketing Manager: Lisa Gordon
Manufacturing and Inventory Control Supervisor: Amy Bacus
Cover Design: Brian Moore
Composition: Cape Cod Compositors, Inc.
Cover Image: © Patricia Vargas/Photos.com
Printing and Binding: Malloy Incorporated
Cover Printing: Malloy Incorporated

Library of Congress Cataloging-in-Publication Data
Thompson, William Norman.
   Ethics in city hall : discussion and analysis for public administration / by William N. Thompson and James E. Leidlein.
      p. cm.
   Includes bibliographical references and index.
   ISBN-13: 978-0-7637-5532-4 (pbk.)
   ISBN-10: 0-7637-5532-X
   1. Municipal officials and employees—Professional ethics—United States.   2. Local government—United States.   3. Political ethics—United States.   I. Leidlein, James E.   II. Title.
   JS401.T46 2008
   172'.2—dc22
                                                                                          2008013287
6048

Printed in the United States of America
12 11 10   10 9 8 7 6 5 4 3 2

Contents

Authors' Acknowledgments   vii

About the Authors   ix

Introduction: It Started Even Before Plato   xi

A Note on the Cases   xv

Chapter 1   The Great Society Gift Horse   1

Discusses the quandary between violating federal hiring rules and employing a questionable person. Examines competing values: safety of children or abiding by the letter of the law.

Chapter 2   Gotta Love Those Bread and Butter Unions   7

Presents the dilemma created when police officers support a candidate for mayor who wins the election. Is the mayor beholden to his supporters' desires even when their police union is concerned about other matters?

Chapter 3   Trust Your Gut or Go with the Flow?   11

Evaluates the hiring of a poorly performing police chief. He was hired under a well-intentioned but flawed selection process and against the intuition of the manager.

Chapter 4   Oh, the Tangled Web We Weave   19

Relates an unfolding drama of a city manager who falsified his credentials when he applied for the position 18 years earlier. Is that long ago action relevant to his qualifications for office now?

Chapter 5   To Tell the Truth   25

Reviews the saga of an incompetent and dishonest community
development director. Should a subordinate be willing to
blow the whistle when a politically motivated governor gives
him a call?

Chapter 6   Dirty Job? Hire a New Person to Do It   31

Demonstrates how something as simple as setting up a
telephone hotline for a large public works project can become
extremely burdensome for a new employee. Is it fair to dump
the job no one wants on the new person?

Chapter 7   A Time for Action—A Time for Reflection   35

Discusses the problem of a police officer who is also a hero
volunteer firefighter. Does his good judgment in one area
make up for bad decisions at other times?

Chapter 8   A Deadly Deed   39

A city and its manager are forced to deal with a situation in
which one of the city's public utility employees runs afoul of
the law. Is a municipality ethically responsible for the
emotional behavior of its employees?

Chapter 9   Punishments to Fit Crimes, But Keep It Quiet   45

Presents a case of blatant plagiarism by a personnel director
while pursuing a graduate degree. Does such behavior
disqualify one for holding a position overseeing the ethics of
others?

Chapter 10   Boss, We've Got a Problem   51

Reviews the challenges faced by a city when it learns that
its popular police youth officer has a hidden secret. Is
it appropriate to keep the investigation from the
governing body?

Chapter 11   Sometimes It's Tough to Explain   57

Discusses difficulty faced in dealing with an injured police
officer who refuses to work.

Chapter 12   Building Inspector: Too Good to Be True   61

Discusses the handling of an aging, incompetent building
inspector whose lack of code enforcement caused problems
for the community, and the hiring of a replacement who
seems just too good to be true.

Chapter 13   Loose Lips Sink Ships and Can Hurt
in Other Ways, Too   69

Evaluates a rivalry between two high-ranking police officers
and why it is so important that confidential investigations not
become part of conversations at office parties.

Chapter 14   Peter, Paul, and Mary: Ethical Quandaries
or Managerial Issues?   73

Discusses the application of the Peter Principle and
considerations of competence in local government politics.

Chapter 15   Elected Officials at Work and/or Play   83

Addresses three situations where a township manager faces
three separate incidences of elected officials patronizing the
world's oldest profession. Are or should elected officials be
held accountable for their moral behavior? Is there a different
standard for appointed officials?

Chapter 16   The Tax Is Illegal—Getting the Story Out   93

Discusses how a township addresses a near 30-year tax levy
and collection that was violative of state law. How do you say
"sorry" to all the taxpayers?

Chapter 17   Betty to the Rescue   99

Evaluates how a high-ranking elected official copes with a
patronage appointee who turns out to be lazy, incompetent,
and a drug user.

Chapter 18   Not Following the Letter of the Law
Is Best Sometimes   105

Discusses the demands of a major taxpayer to have its property
assessment significantly reduced. Is a plea that the company may
have to close its doors viable at tax assessing time?

Chapter 19   Because of Good Intergovernmental
Relations, Some Things Could Be Buried Quickly   111

Evaluates how good intentions regarding the purchase of
property for a cemetery by township officials can go awry,
and how good relations with fellow governments can help hide
some unethical activity.

Chapter 20   The Rarest of the Rare   117

Explores the trials and tribulations of a community and
its local government dealing with an employee and his
family whose 10-year-old daughter is dying from an
incurable disease.

Chapter 21   Hire the Hard-Core Unemployed   129

When one hires someone, one may have that someone for a
very long time. Shows the downside of the C.E.T.A. program
that funded hiring the hard-core unemployed.

Appendix I   Codes of Ethics   139

Appendix II   Sometimes Choices Can Be Difficult   149

Appendix III A Bitter Taste on the Lips   151

Appendix IV Annotated Bibliography of Selected Books   153

Appendix V   A Selected List of Films on Ethics   163

Index   169

Authors' Acknowledgments

Author **William Thompson** thanks his wife, Kay, for her support and for enduring moments not only of writing but also the consternation over unfolding events in several of the cases presented.

Author **James Leidlein** acknowledges the help and support of his wife, Kathleen, and his children, Catherine, David, Eric, and Katrina and her husband, Scott, for the trials and tribulations associated with the studies presented here and others yet to be written. Fellow city managers will recognize the importance of family support as they address difficult and challenging issues faced often in their daily lives.

Both authors want to recognize their students at University of Nevada–Las Vegas and Wayne State University in Detroit for engaging in discussions about the cases and offering useful insight into their composition and presentation. They would also like to express their thanks and gratitude to the staff at Jones and Bartlett, especially Jeremy Spiegel, Lisa Gordon, Julia Waugaman, and Maro Asadoorian for their very kind and helpful assistance.

William N. Thompson, PhD—Professor, University of Nevada–Las Vegas,
  Las Vegas, Nevada

William N. Thompson is a Professor of Public Administration at the University of Nevada–Las Vegas. He was born and raised in Ann Arbor, Michigan, and attended Michigan State University and the University of Missouri at Columbia, receiving a PhD (Political Science) from the latter in 1972. He has taught Political Science and Public Administration courses at Southeast Missouri State, Western Michigan University, Troy State University (Europe), and the University of Nevada–Las Vegas. He served as a research associate with the National Association of Attorneys General, a research advisor of Pension and Welfare Benefits in the United States Department of Labor, and as the elected supervisor of Kalamazoo Charter Township, Michigan. His research interests have focused upon many public policy questions with an emphasis on policy and the gambling industry. His books include *Gambling in America: An Encyclopedia, Legalized Gambling: A Reference Handbook, Native American Issues: A Reference Handbook,* and *The Last Resort: Success and Failure in Campaigns for Casinos* (with John Dombrink). His articles have appeared in many academic, professional, and trade journals, including *Public Integrity, Gaming Law Review,* and *Casino Lawyer.* His commentaries on gambling issues have been quoted by national media such as *The New York Times, Washington Post,* and *Wall Street Journal,* and he has appeared on the *Today Show, Crossfire, The O'Reilly Factor,* and *Marketplace.*

James E. Leidlein, MPA—City Manager, City of Harper Woods, Harper Woods,
  Michigan

James Leidlein has been a city manager in Michigan for over 30 years. He was also employed as a labor economist with the U.S. Department of Labor in Washington, D.C. He earned an undergraduate degree in Business Administration from Western Michigan University and a graduate degree in Public Administration from the University of Southern California. He has been an adjunct faculty member in the Political Science Department at Wayne State University in Detroit for 20 years. He has taught introductory courses in American Government and Public Administration and graduate classes in Labor Relations and Administrative Ethics. He has been published in *Public Administration Review, Public Integrity,* and is cited in *Public Personnel Management* and Berkley and Rouse's *The Craft of Public Administration.* He is also a member of the Michigan Local Government Management Association's Ethics Committee. He resides with his wife, Kathleen, in Harper Woods, Michigan.

It Started Even Before Plato

Ethically competent decision making constitutes that central value system of Plato's *Republic*. Plato grew to adulthood in an Athenian society that was built upon the foundation of equality and majority rule, values somewhat at odds with those expressed in the *Republic*. Plato had a mentor. His name was Socrates, and he challenged the wisdom of a political system that chose its leaders by using a lottery (how more equal could the selection of officials be?), and made its decisions by having the totality of all eligible citizens gather at a city square and cast majority votes on each of many issues set on the agenda for each periodic town meeting.

Socrates was critical that this mass democracy led to bad decisions made on the spur of the moment, often emotionally and without serious substantive debate or deliberation. Socrates called the process of leadership and lawmaking, "government by street cleaners." He offered a contrary notion that public decisions should be made by the wisest citizens through extensive study into all aspects of the subject matter concerned. While advocating this alternative system, Socrates was cutting in his criticism of what he considered incompetence and even corruption by the lottery winners and street cleaners. Socrates was criticizing the central value system of democracy, and as a result the leaders of Athens decided to put him on trial for corrupting the youth.

A majority of the citizens in the town square found Socrates guilty as charged. A minority felt he was clearly within his rights to be critical of the political process, but the Athenian democracy was a majority rule system, not a process that had minority rights. The sentence was simple enough: Socrates was merely ordered to stop his criticism. But Socrates refused the sentence. There was no appeal, no Supreme Court, no review and alternative sentencing. Either a convicted party accepted the punishment of the officials in charge, or he had to accept exile from the community. The problem was that Socrates loved Athens; he had never lived anywhere else, and all his family and friends were in Athens. He refused to leave. There was another way to be exiled. He could "leave" by accepting death. This he willingly did in what was perhaps the most dramatic exercise of civil disobedience recorded up to that time. He requested a pitcher filled with hemlock poison, and he drank it.

Plato[1] reacted to Socrates's death by making Socrates the model for a class of leaders called "philosopher kings" who would rule the public realms of his mythical republic. All citizens from birth would be educated together in public schools. They would be taught all subjects, especially moral and ethical subjects, and they would be given many examinations. At age 18 they would take a life examination. They would then be divided into three classes. Some would be artisans—workers; another group would be protectors—warriors. The third group would become guardians, and the best of these eventually would become philosopher kings. The guardians would receive an intense college-like liberal arts education, and they would always be subject to examinations to test their moral character. At the end of their education they would serve many years as administrators of governmental departments. Their successful careers would then lead to their appointment as philosopher kings.

Making a wise and moral leader involved more than just training. Plato was concerned that outside evil forces would always be tugging at a leader, beckoning the leader to make a wrong step. One force was greed and the desire to possess things. It was all right to have these desires, but if they controlled one's behavior, the person was better off as an artisan, where the enjoyment of personal stuff need not interfere with the public well being. The members of Plato's guardian class passed practical exams that demonstrated their resistance to the pull of having lots of stuff. Also, when they entered the guardian class, they were forever restricted from having private property. They took a virtual vow of poverty, and the government provided for their basic housing and other needs. They would not be corrupted by greed for things.

Plato was concerned about lust. Lust had been known to have led a leader or two astray even back then in ancient times (Plato lived approximately 427 BC–347 BC). Not only could the guardians and philosopher kings not have property, but they could not have exclusive partners, either. The guardians instead would have temporary arranged marriages for purposes of procreation and limited companionship. They would be spied upon by agents of their leaders to assure their fidelity to the rules, and to assure that their decision making would not be influenced by improper

---

[1]See Rice, Daryl. *A Guide to Plato's Republic*. New York: Oxford University Press, 1998.

alliances. The strong force of nepotism was countered by the fact that all babies born in the Republic would be separated from their birth parents and raised in communes by others. They did not know their parentage (although the high leaders kept records), and hence when in positions of decision making and influence they could not be pulled by consideration of family ties over the need to serve the common good. The power of organizational loyalty and organizational friendships was checked by an administrative system that demanded that guardians change the departments in which they served every few years as they progressed upwards in the system.

The corrupting influence of power was recognized. However, Plato took stark exception to the words of British Lord Acton who had said (over 2,000 years later), "Power corrupts; absolute power corrupts absolutely."[2] Plato found that the corrupting nature of power was found in a leader's desire for more power; when more power was achieved, the leader then wanted more power. Plato saw this as a vicious cycle that would only be broken if the leader was given all the power that there was. "Power corrupts, but absolute power checks the corrupting influence of power." Plato assigned absolute power to one philosopher king who sat at the top of the hierarchy. All of the decisions of this philosopher king would be final. All issues in dispute would be brought to this philosopher king. This philosopher king could impose his or her will upon any guardian working in the public domain.

When a person ascended to the position of philosopher king, it was somewhat like a full professor at a university being given a reverse sabbatical. A sabbatical at a university is typically a 1-year period of grace with no work requirements. Sabbatical years are given to professors each 7 years of teaching work. Here the philosopher kings had perpetual sabbaticals during which time they could study, read, contemplate poetry, and just sit around having wonderful thoughts and working out mathematical equations. But, in that 1 year—the special year, actually for a time of but a month—they would be called out of their ivory tower status and recruited to be *the* philosopher king in charge. They were quite happy when their term of absolute power ended.

Modern codes of ethics borrow ideas from Plato's *Republic*, fictional society though it was. However, the codes also adhere to notions extant in the democratic value structure of Athens as well; for instance, all voices on the street corner, even those of the uneducated deserve to be heard. Codes accept the idea that all citizens, not just those of one class, deserve respect, and that the majority will must be part of the public fabric. Codes go further and incorporate aspects of later democracies that emphasize due process and the need to protect minorities in society.

The actions taken by officials and others in the cases presented in this book are meant to be criticized with an analysis fitting one given by Athenians—both the

---

[2]See Hirsch, Jr., E.D., Kett, Joseph F., and Trefil, James, eds. *The New Dictionary of Cultural Literacy*. 3rd ed. Boston: Houghton Mifflin, 2002.

street corner democrats and the students of Socrates. They are to be measured against more modern codes of ethics as well. Readers are to ask—were the decision makers in the cases wise people; were they moral; did they respect the individuals who stood before them; did they respect all of the citizens? Did they do the right thing; did they do the wrong thing? If they did the wrong thing, how could they have changed their actions for the better? Many actions were taken outside of the sunshine of openness. Were officials justified in acting in such a manner? Were the officials required to take all private matters concerning the public good to a public forum? Some of the cases may appear not to involve ethical matters. The reader is asked to consider if such is really the case. Situations involving incompetence raise the question of whether it is ethical to permit recurring incompetence by subordinates for some perhaps humanitarian motive, such as the employee was loyal for so many years that superiors hesitate to force him out. One interesting question comes up time and again. The reader should ask if bad decision making is justified if it is done with good intentions, and not done to enrich undeserving parties. Several times leaders take actions that are contrary to some rule or required process. In some cases leaders actually violate laws by their actions. Is it ever right for a leader to do so? Can a public official ever be justified in breaking the law?

At the onset we have described in very scanty detail aspects of democracy in Athens and some provisions of Plato's *Republic*. With the permission of the American Society for Public Administration and the International City/County Management Association (ICMA), we have placed their codes of ethics in this book. We do so in Appendix I.

A Note on the Cases

The stories told in the 21 cases presented in this book are true stories. That is, each main story line presented is true; it actually happened, somewhere, some place, at some time. Real people were involved, and they took the actions we describe. The authors know many of the people involved in the stories. In some cases, their colleagues have shared their stories with the authors. However, in each case, the names of places and the names of people involved have been changed. This will be obvious to some readers who may recognize events and fictional names presented. Some of the actors involved remain in office today; others left office 2 decades ago or longer. Some have died. The stories are meant to be illustrations of activities that actually occur and that deserve to be analyzed from a perspective of ethics and good decision making.

The authors have not pledged to conceal any of the identities of the places and the actors involved in these case studies, but we intend to do so. If you think you know a place, don't ask. If you do ask, we are each certain that it was a case the other knew about, or maybe it was a case a colleague brought to us. Instead of seeking such unimportant truths, we urge you to seek wisdom in codes of ethics and models of liberties and public will and competence as you seek answers to your own case studies in the ones presented in the book.

Each of the stories reported took place in a village, town, township, or city with a population between 10,000 and 40,000. All took place over the past 30 years.

The case studies are not designed in order to have readers reflect on policy issues, although some situations with policy issue content are presented in the appendices as supplemental stories. For this reason we hope that the reader will not assign any political or partisan or philosophical bias to the authors. In truth, we do not always agree with each other on policy issues and how we would vote in particular local, state, and national elections. One is no doubt more conservative and the other more liberal, but those philosophies are not concerns with the cases presented. We are not looking at the life and death issues of war, capital punishment, or abortion, or whether or not to eat meat or wear fur, or use products with chemicals that may or may not harm the environment, or may have been the end result of exploitive labor systems. Nor are we looking at major issues in debates over tax equity or expenditures for education or poverty programs or programs to deal with societal equity and discrimination. This is not a macro-policy analysis book. Ethically, that may be good, or that may be bad, but that is reality. Rather, this is a book that is focused upon rather mundane situations involving questions about right and wrong behavior of individuals—asking questions about how you and I should react to real situations that could be thrust into our faces every day—and quite frankly *are* pushed into our faces every day.

One theme in many of the stories is that important issues often appear at the doorstep unannounced. An official can drive to the office expecting a routine day, only to receive a knock at the door. In comes a brush fire that could lead to a forest fire. So many brush fires. Both authors have had extensive government and teaching experience. One author left the uncertainties of the lifestyle of a brush firefighter and went back to the classroom to get his daily paycheck. The other has taught extensively, but instead of pursuing a teaching career, he has opted to remain a full-time public administrator for over 3 decades. They have served with local, state, and federal governments or governmental associations. They were once in the same classroom together, one as a professor and the other as a student. They also served together at the same time in the United States Department of Labor, under presidents Gerald Ford and Jimmy Carter. Their positions have included both elected and appointed offices. This raises one last question: should elected officials be subjected to different ethical guidelines than appointed officials?

The teaching method encompassed in the presentation of materials in this book is not one of furnishing the answers to the question of what is right or wrong in particular situations. We are seeking instead to have the reader analyze the situations and behaviors presented, and then reflect on how one should deal with the circumstances involved. If the reader is in public service, the reader knows that these and similar circumstances do arise quite often. If the reader is a student contemplating a career in any organization, the reader is on notice—he or she will confront ethical quandaries and dilemmas; that's just life. Read on!

Chapter 1

The Great Society Gift Horse

"Never let your sense of morals get in the way of doing what's right."

—Isaac Asimov

William T. Gamble was elected to the post of township supervisor in 1978. The full-time position entailed duties such as property assessment, general administration of staff, and service as chair of the board of trustees. The board consisted of seven elected individuals, four citizen (part-time) trustees, and the full-time supervisor, clerk, and treasurer. The supervisor was considered the policy leader of the township government.

Gamble knew the board was conservative, indeed he shared their antitax, antispend point of view. All seven were Republicans. He was the only new member of the board following the 1978 election. He soon found out what conservative meant in action.

Grand Prairie Road was only 1 mile long. However, along its course there were several houses, an elementary school and its yard, a golf course, and a public park. There was no sidewalk on either side of Grand Prairie. This presented a problem for the children, as Gamble knew. Two of his children attended the school. Many of the schoolchildren walked to school along Grand Prairie, and as they walked they found themselves either walking on the grass in front of the homes or park, or they found themselves walking in the street. The latter case was typical in wintertime as road maintenance crews plowed snow onto the grass as they cleared the roadway. This presented a danger to the children, although there was no record of a child being hit by a car while walking to or from school.

Gamble often thought about the danger facing the children, but he never thought he could do anything about it before. As an elected official, he could. He took office in November, and found himself confronted with many other issues. But in the springtime his mind turned to this concern once more. He had received a few inquiries from parents about the same safety concerns, but unfortunately, he had received some other phone calls as well. Several homeowners who lived on Grand Prairie called to complain about the schoolchildren walking on their lawns. They told Gamble that he should order the township police to patrol the area and to order the children off the lawns and onto the street. Before he was elected, Gamble would have returned an earful to these complainers, whom he felt to be very selfish people. But now he listened, and he let them know that he would be looking into the matter. He felt he had to make an effort to have sidewalks built on at least one side of Grand Prairie. With a school crossing guard in front of the school, this would offer a good solution to everyone's concern.

Gamble informally discussed building a sidewalk with the clerk and treasurer, as he did most other issues as they arose. If he were taking a matter to the board, he wanted to have their opinions, and he always wanted their support. Both these officials told him that the township had a very set procedure in these cases. Sidewalks would be built by the township only if a majority of homeowners on a street filed a petition with the township requesting the sidewalks. The homeowners would then be billed the cost of building the sidewalks. They suggested that he follow the procedure and contact the homeowners. Gamble was doubtful that this was a solution, but he agreed to take the first step. He drew up the petitions and he went to the street and knocked on all the doors. It was an exercise in futility. Not a single homeowner signed the petition. They were unanimous in their opposition to the sidewalk, especially to the idea that they pay for the sidewalks. They didn't have any children going to that school. And they loved how their grass would go all the way to the street. A sidewalk would hurt the look of their lawns and maybe the value of their property. While the township clearly owned the land alongside the street, the homeowners took pride of ownership, and wanted no sidewalks.

Gamble's next step would be to take the matter to the township board. Here the clerk and treasurer indicated that he would have a difficult time. In no way was the board going to order a sidewalk to be built and to make the homeowners pay against their opposition. Each of the other board members had gone through three elections or more and this was no way to win votes. The clerk and treasurer showed sympathy with the idea of a sidewalk, but they didn't feel that the board would go along with the idea of having the township pay for a sidewalk either. Nonetheless, they told Gamble that it might be worth taking the time for a discussion of the matter, and so the item was placed on the agenda of the next board meeting.

At the board meeting, there was general agreement that a sidewalk would be good for Grand Prairie Road, even if the homeowners did not want one. They also agreed that the children benefiting from the sidewalks would not be children living in the homes along the road. However they were unanimous in the opinion that the township should not pay for the sidewalks, and that the township should not build sidewalks against the will of the homeowners and then make them pay for them. One member suggested that the homeowners could even sue if this was done. All agreed that either action would be a bad precedent. Time-honored words filled the air: "We've never done it that way before; I don't know why we should start doing it that way now." Trustees expressed the notion that if they changed their ways others would complain, and soon everyone would want them to build sidewalks in front of their houses for free. Gamble felt stymied. He declined to bring the matter to any kind of vote, choosing instead to pass on to the next agenda item. He was happy that he had that prerogative in that he was the chair of the board.

Being a government official is always a learning experience, and Gamble was learning that much of his job involved intergovernmental relations. One day he received a call from a federal government official requesting an appointment. She was from the Labor Department's Comprehensive Employment Training Administration—C.E.T.A. for short. The official who was in the local C.E.T.A. field office explained that C.E.T.A. could provide employees free of charge to the township if the township had projects that would be valuable for their job training. Gamble started turning the wheels in his brain thinking of projects. "Bingo," he said to himself, "the sidewalk!"

Gamble formulated the concept in his head and took the idea to his colleagues, the treasurer, and clerk.

They agreed that he might sell the board on the idea of building the sidewalk if the labor was free—or mostly free, if the township would only have to provide equipment (which they already had) and the cement—a small part of the cost of the sidewalk. The township would also have to provide one person to give training assistance and on-site supervision. Before attempting to sell the idea to the board, he wrote up the proposal for a C.E.T.A. project that would involve five federally-funded workers for 3 months of labor. He then shared the idea with the C.E.T.A. official. She endorsed the idea and said the project could start as soon as the township made an official application. That required board action.

This time the treasurer and clerk endorsed the idea, and the trustees only grumbled. They had been informed of the C.E.T.A. program, and they indicated that they would go along, although a few made negative comments about the bad precedent they would be setting. As chair, Gamble called for a voice vote, and hearing no vocal objections, he declared the matter passed. The project was rolling.

The C.E.T.A. hiring procedures were simple. The federal agency had a list of eligible employees, and they selected candidates for the jobs. They would then send the job applicants to the township supervisor one by one. The supervisor would then interview the candidates. Afterwards, he would indicate that the township was hiring the applicant or it was not hiring the applicant. This had to be done before another applicant would be sent for an interview. If the applicant was turned down for the job, the township had to fill out a report for the C.E.T.A. office indicating precisely why the applicant was turned down. As part of the interview process the applicant could be asked to have a back X-ray taken, as the job required physical work. This would protect the township against workman's compensation claims for injuries that might have preexisted.

The first applicant seemed to be fit for the job, and after he passed his X-ray test, the township indicated that he was being hired. Then the second applicant was interviewed. He was a young man who looked to be in great physical shape. His resumé indicated that he had held several jobs, although at the time of the interview, he was unemployed. The record also indicated a 2-year period with no job experience and no education experience. As was appropriate for the interview process, Gamble asked him what he was doing during those 2 years. The young man simply said, "prison." The rules of the game were quite simple at this point; Gamble was prohibited from making any further inquiry into this matter. He knowingly violated the rules and asked one word, "Where?" The young man could have refused to answer, but instead said one word, "Jackson." Jackson was the state's maximum security prison. Gamble then instructed the man to have his back X-ray taken.

Gamble crossed his fingers just hoping against hope that the young man would fail the back examination. Gamble's hopes were dashed. The young man passed the examination. Gamble was in a quandary. He knew right from wrong, and he knew the hiring laws. He had done all that he was permitted to do—and more as well. He had already violated legal interviewing procedures.

Gamble decided to talk to a man he supervised, the chief of the township police department. The chief heard him out, and said only, "Sorry, I'm not your man." Gamble begged. He asked the chief if his computer could access records about ex-convicts. The chief told Gamble, "You know it can." He added, "That, Mr. Gamble, would be a felony." He indicated to the supervisor that he had been appointed chief of police in order to uphold the law, not to break the law. Gamble and the chief just sat for about 5 minutes without a word being spoken between them. Gamble then suggested that he could type a name in the computer if the correct program was accessed. They sat outside the open door of the computer room. The chief said something to the effect of, "Look, get out of here, and don't come back if I'm here. I'm going to be gone for lunch for the next hour."

Gamble left the chief's office, but he returned in 10 minutes. The chief was gone, and the computer was on, with the cursor at a square that indicated: "name." Gamble typed in the name. He looked down the file of convictions. Felonies. Maximum security punishment. The words came up: "Child sexual molestation." Gamble turned the computer off.

Gamble thought of the saying, "I'm from the federal government, and I'm here to help you." Supervisor Gamble had asked C.E.T.A. for workers to build a sidewalk beside an elementary school. They sent applicants. One was a convicted sexual molester of children.

Gamble was handed a choice. He could hire the applicant, or he could turn the applicant down. If he did the latter, he would have to declare why he was denying employment to the applicant. But to tell why would involve confession to committing a felony—misuse of confidential police equipment and violation of privacy rights and inappropriate hiring procedures. What was Gamble to do?

Gamble really wanted to build the sidewalk. Was there any way he could hire the young man knowing what he knew? He reasoned that they could have the maintenance crew member in charge of the workers spend all his time watching the one worker. But would that really work? Was there any way he could turn the young man down? What kind of reason could he give? The township had other ex-convicts in its employment. Prison time in and of itself was not a reason to turn down a job applicant. But could he tell the truth?

Gamble decided he could not tell the truth. He also told himself that his lawbreaking activity involved a violation of a law of man, not a law of God. He told himself that he could sleep at night knowing what he had done. Yet he wanted to keep what he had done to himself. Even the chief did not know exactly what he had done, or if he had done anything with the computer at all, although he might have wondered who turned the computer off. For all he knew Gamble turned the computer off without looking up the name.

At the next board meeting Gamble approached two of the trustees who had been most outspoken against the sidewalk project. He asked them if they still felt the same. They indicated that they did.

Later Gamble talked with the clerk and treasurer and told them he was uncomfortable with the project because he knew that there was still serious opposition to it. He very discreetly indicated the nature of his problem to the clerk and asked if it would be all right to tell C.E.T.A. that they were canceling the project because of persistent opposition among some members of the board. The clerk agreed that that would be a good course to take. The C.E.T.A. official was somewhat upset, but Gamble indicated that the township had a couple of office projects, as he apologized for the political situation at the township. The C.E.T.A. official indicated that she understood how tricky local government politics could get. The project was canceled.

Questions

1. Was this a good ending for the problem presented in the case? Is there any way the sidewalk could have been built?
2. Consider if the supervisor would have done anything differently if his children did not attend the school. How might Gamble have felt if a car had hit a child on the road in front of the school?

3. Is it ever ethical to break the law? Even if it is not a felony? Was Gamble correct that laws of men and laws of God can be treated differently? Would a jury have agreed with this had actions been taken to court?

4. Would the police chief and township clerk have been subject to legal penalties if Gamble would have been prosecuted?

5. Should the C.E.T.A. officials share some responsibility for putting the supervisor into his dilemma situation?

Chapter 2

Gotta Love Those Bread and Butter Unions

"Leadership is a potent combination of strategy and character. But if you must be without one, be without strategy."

—Norman Schwarzkopf

Mayor Perry Burns won an election to head the Sealy City government with the active support of the Sealy Law Enforcement Officers' Association. Two of the Sealy policemen had been students of Burns, whose daytime job had been as a professor of public administration at Woodside State College. The police force agreed to make yard signs and get them posted throughout the city. They paid all the expenses for the signs, while Burns gathered funds for other campaign efforts. Burns also agreed to knock on every door in the city of 25,000. There were about 10,000 doors.

Burns ran against a three-term incumbent who had made enemies while in office. His major problem was that he drank excessively and often while on the job. Burns was very fortunate that a third person ran. The third person was known as a hot head, and he used the incumbent's alcoholism as his major issue. Burns had the best of both worlds. He could absolutely refuse to discuss the incumbent's personal behavior and focused instead on leadership issues. The third person in the race did the dirty work. The only issue his opponents had against Burns was that he was a professor. Somehow that meant he wasn't in some real world where the uneducated lived. The fact the police were visibly helping him pretty much killed that issue.

The police, or at least the two policemen who had been Burns's students, had an agenda. They strongly disliked the police chief. They fancied the notion that Burns would be able to rein in the chief. The unspoken desire was that Burns would fire the chief. There was no question in Burns's mind that he won the election because of the help he received from the police and their union. He felt obligated.

Soon after taking office, Burns realized that the other members of the city council, and the other citywide elected officials—the clerk and the treasurer, actually liked the police chief. They were not even neutral. They were positive about the chief. They pointed out to Burns that the chief was a no-nonsense guy who demanded discipline from the officers, and he also demanded that the policemen (and three policewomen) look sharp. City residents also expressed pleasure about the crisp uniforms and clean cars and good manners of their police. Burns had been to college; he even taught at a college. He could count. Any effort on his part to fire the chief would result in a six to one vote against Burns. He would have to bide his time. As the months went by, he continued to have selected policemen come to him to complain about the chief's arbitrary behavior, his favoritism toward certain officers, and his mean disposition. Burns always kept the door open. He even occasionally went to a local bar when members of the police force hung out.

Burns was uneasy, and the unease did increase a bit when his two close acquaintances on the force resigned and both moved to Florida to pursue a business venture. When he heard complaints, he tried to get the policemen making the complaints to propose some kind of solutions, to at least give some options for him to consider. Those were indeed rare, although he still heard the notion expressed that things would get better if they had a different chief.

The police had a collective bargaining contract that had a 2-year term. Eight months into the mayor's term, the contract expired. A month before that time, the clerk informed the mayor that they would have to form a bargaining team. The mayor knew he was in a potential conflict of interest situation, so he informed the clerk that he should not be on the team. The clerk would have none of it. He said, "Look, it is very appropriate for the police to be involved in campaigns for the mayor's office. After all, almost all of them live in the city. But that is no reason you cannot do your job on the negotiating board and represent all the citizens—not just the police." The mayor agreed that he could, but he also told the clerk that he liked the police force. The clerk said that was O.K., that that was good. The mayor, the clerk, and two city council members were chosen by the entire board to be the bargaining team for the government.

The mayor knew it was a bit out of order, but he took the risk anyway. He told a couple of policemen who were active in the union that his general disposition favored the policemen, but that he was representing all the citizens. He added that he had heard much about the police force since taking office and even before, and that the bargaining process might just be a place to put some issues on the table. The policemen said not to worry; they knew what to put on the table.

The union asked for an allowance for cleaning their uniforms. However, it was a time of double-digit inflation, so everyone expected that salary money would be the big bargaining issue. It was. Indeed, when the police asked the board what they would give, the city board said, "You can have what you have now and a 4% increase each of the next 2 years."

The cries went up, "My God! Attila the Hun. You are Neanderthals." "Unrealistic." "Slave Labor." And so it went.

After about 15 minutes of howling, the city board said, "Here it is, take it or leave it. Leave it, and we go to arbitration."

The union representatives said, "We want 15% this year and 15% next year."

The city board was stunned and decided to go home for the night. They suspected they were heading for arbitration.

That evening the city officials seemed to think that the sky was falling, but the mayor was able to corner a policeman not on the bargaining team. The mayor told him that he was surprised that the union had not raised any issues about the chief's conduct. The policeman said, "Look, we want the money."

The next morning the clerk gathered the mayor together with the treasurer and the two council members. He had spent the night over the books, and he figured that without any tax increases or decreases in the surplus fund the city could afford to give the policemen 12% that year and 10% the next year. He suggested tying the 10% to the inflation rate—making 10% a maximum. The mayor was pleasantly stunned. All discussed the matter and agreed that that would be their counterproposal, and they would throw in the cleaning allowance, also.

The union representatives returned to the bargaining table expecting to demand arbitration and then to walk out. The clerk asked if they would like to hear a counterproposal. They agreed. When they heard "12%," they were pleasantly surprised.

When they heard the full proposal, they agreed to take the proposal to the members.

Two days later the police union voted 29–1 to accept the contract. The bargaining process had saved the mayor's butt. He could finally sleep at night without feeling that he had let his friends—his campaigners—down. They didn't really hate the chief; he was just a symbol. A good enough symbol to get Burns elected, but not a big enough symbol to deter the union from its bread and butter concerns—salaries. Burns could also adopt a new posture toward policemen who came to him to gripe. He could then suggest they take their issues to their union steward.

Questions

1. Did Burns turn his back on the people who elected him?
2. Was it proper for Burns to serve on the city's bargaining board?

3. Was it proper for Burns to hint that the police union put concerns about the chief on the bargaining table?

4. Did the union really represent the police force well? Should they have asked for more?

5. Was Burns really on the police side of the bargaining table?

Chapter 3

Trust Your Gut or Go with the Flow?

"Conventionality is not morality."

—Charlotte Brontë

"You were hired on a four–three vote and I wasn't one of the four" an obviously agitated mayor told the newly appointed city manager. "You've got 6 months to prove yourself, and if you don't, you will be fired," he added emphatically. Fresh out of graduate school and slated to be the youngest city manager in the state, Jack Ellis was excited, nonetheless, with his appointment to the position with the city of Woodside.

With an elected mayor, clerk, treasurer, and four aldermen, Ellis was only the second manager of Woodside and its first professional one. The previous manager had a background in auto sales. He was a friend of three-term Mayor Marvin Morris, who had essentially run the city for the past 6 years. The mayor had a hand-picked replacement lined up for the departing manager (who had resigned for unknown reasons) in the form of the deputy police chief, Bob Collins. Morris and the former manager had hired the deputy chief directly over the police chief's objection. Police Chief Ronald Grover and Mayor Morris did not see eye to eye, and the fact that the city council passed over Collins for the manager's slot strained the relationship even more. There was also a race issue. Chief Grover was a large

African American. Mayor Morris was what many described as a white bigot, a label many also gave to Deputy Chief Collins.

Woodside was a city with a population of just over 10,000 compacted into an area just slightly over 1 square mile. It was adjacent to Vernon, a larger central city of about 90,000 people. While portions of Woodside fit the definition of the traditional suburb, most of it was simply a spillover from the larger urban community, and the boundaries were nearly invisible. It had a significant minority population with 65% black, 10% Hispanic, and the remainder white (the usual minority was the majority in Woodside). It was also severely impoverished. Over half of its residents lived in poverty and were on some form of public assistance. The city's development in the 1950s and 1960s reflected typical racist patterns of the times. Water and sewer mains bypassed poorer black neighborhoods to serve more affluent white neighborhoods.

With poverty comes high unemployment and with that comes high crime, or so it seems. Woodside had all that and then some. It averaged an incredible one homicide a month. While more often than not the crime itself occurred in Vernon, the victim's remains were dumped in open fields in Woodside and became a crime statistic in Woodside. The twenty-one member police department was a busy one. As a likely result of discriminatory hiring practices in the 1960s, the department's racial makeup did not reflect the community's significant minority population. Only three officers were black, none were Hispanic, and no females claimed membership on the force. Of the three blacks, one was Chief Grover, who had risen in the ranks from officer to sergeant and then chief. How he became chief is a matter of debate (Woodside had no civil service system) but it was at the orchestration of Mayor Morris and the auto-salesman city manager about 3 years prior to City Manager's Ellis's arrival. Many believed that the mayor made an African American police chief in an effort to dispel his white bigot image.

Despite his appointment of Grover, Grover and the mayor continued to butt heads. The mayor was a very hands-on one. In his private vehicle, he had a fully functional police radio and often would communicate with patrol cars directly. He would issue orders, direct their activities, and be very active when he was out and about. He showed up at nearly every homicide scene for a first-hand look. While Chief Grover did not care for this there was not much he could do about it. The city manager was simply a pawn of the mayor so complaining to him would fall of deaf ears.

The mayor was not very satisfied with the chief's management style either, and thus hired Collins, a police lieutenant in another community police agency, and made him deputy chief. Mayor Morris directed Collins to straighten out the department. Chief Grover had no say in the creation of the position or the hiring of Collins. This created quite a schism in the police department and, to a lesser extent, the community. Both Grover and Collins had their supporters and detractors, but the chief would win out in the community. Being black helped, but he was an outgoing, gregarious character. He was a glad hander who charmed almost everyone with whom he came into contact. His attendance at community events was always well received and he rarely missed any of them.

Deputy Chief Collins was somewhat the opposite. He came across as stern and gruff. He was a policeman's policeman. While not a recluse, when he did attend community events, he usually only made a brief appearance. While his police experience and credentials far exceeded those of the chief (whose only qualifying experience when he applied to the department was that of an ex-marine), Collins did not have the community support.

This did not deter Mayor Morris from pushing for Collins's appointment as city manager when the vacancy arose. In an effort to limit competition for the manager's position, it was only advertised locally. Only fifteen or so people applied, one being Ellis, who lived in another state. He learned of the city manager's vacancy from a family member who lived in another suburb of Vernon. Although the mayor had secured the four votes for Collins, he felt compelled to go through the motion of conducting interviews with three finalists: Collins, Ellis, and a local attorney. After the second round of interviews, a motion was made to appoint Collins and the confident Marvin Morris was assured that he had performed his magic. But when the vote was taken, the treasurer had changed his mind and cast the deciding *no* vote. It was learned later that the treasurer changed his vote at the eleventh hour because he felt the mayor had too much power. A motion was then made to hire Ellis and passed by the slim 4–3 margin. The infuriated mayor called Ellis at his hotel and issued the 6-month ultimatum.

Eager to begin his career in city management, Jack Ellis enthusiastically walked into the position with his eyes "wide shut." He was unaware of the politics surrounding his appointment or the ongoing feud between the mayor and police chief. He did learn early on that Deputy Chief Collins was not only disappointed but bitter over losing out on the manager's post. But no one was more bitter over the power struggle than the mayor. If his boy could not be the manager then, by golly, he was going to be the city's next police chief. His next mission was to get rid of Chief Grover.

In his first 3 months as manager, Ellis succumbed to the mayor's pressure and followed him around like a puppy dog, including appearances at three homicides. The mayor had a small office at city hall, which he visited precisely at 4:30 each day when he got off of his full-time job as a maintenance worker at a printing shop. He would sit at his desk and write several AVO's, which were 3″×5″ yellow pads of paper with the bold heading "Avoid Verbal Orders." He would write directives on these separate slips of form paper and give them to the city manager. Ellis quickly grew to despise these yellow slips of paper.

The mayor would regularly vent his displeasure with the police chief to the city manager, often times shrouded in racial innuendo. He felt that Chief Grover was incompetent, barbaric, bombastic, and, because of his girth, an embarrassment to the city. He continued his close association with the deputy chief and others in the department to undermine Grover. While City Manager Ellis saw the mayor on a daily basis, he only saw the other elected officials at their bimonthly council meetings. The council, however, noticed that their new, young city manager was acting more like an assistant to the mayor, and this did not sit well with them. Ellis was reminded that he worked for the entire council, especially the four-member majority that appointed him. As such, after a few months he began to distance himself from the mayor and became more independent and assertive.

He actually found Grover to be an effective and competent police chief who certainly had the support of the community and a majority of the city council. The three-member minority, including the mayor, wanted him gone. Like anyone, the chief certainly had his weaknesses, but overall the manager thought his performance was good.

After working together for about a year, the police chief approached the city manager with a request. He needed to take a 2-month unpaid leave of absence to tend to his elderly mother, who was terminally ill. Ellis granted the request. The chief asked that he still be allowed to use his city vehicle during his absence as he would respond to emergencies if needed. The manager granted that request as well.

When Mayor Morris learned of this he was incensed—outright livid. He told the city manager that the chief was probably lying about his mother's illness. The mayor was proved wrong when she died 8 weeks later. Morris demanded that the chief return the car to police headquarters and park it there during his leave. He also directed the manager to make Deputy Chief Collins the acting police chief. The manager refused, arguing that filling in for the chief when he is absent is exactly what a deputy does. This did not sit well with the mayor, either.

At the next city council meeting, the mayor went ballistic. He conceded that it was probably within the manager's authority to grant the chief's leave, but allowing him to use a city car during his leave was another thing altogether. Morris felt it was a travesty and outright wrong. After his tirade, he was successful in garnering three votes to join his in overruling the manager. Such local government drama often piqued the interest of the local news media, and this was no exception. It made the local 11:00 news, with an on-camera appearance by a visibly upset mayor. He stated to the news reporter, "Here is yet another example of Chief Grover trying to steal from the city."[1] At 11:15, the telephone rang at city manager Ellis's home.

It was an emphatic, "I quit!" call from Chief Grover. Despite valiant efforts, Ellis could not change the chief's mind. The mayor had won once again. It appeared that opportunity had once again knocked for Deputy Chief Bob Collins . . . or had it?

Mr. Ellis certainly had his feet to the proverbial fire. His first appointment in his young career was that of a police chief. There is something about police chiefs that garner the media's attention. It may be due to the nature of the job or the type of individual attracted to it. Nothing pleases a reporter more than the opportunity to write about an embattled police chief. In what was to come, they would nearly run out of ink in the printing press of Woodside.

Perhaps the easy thing for the city manager to do would have been to simply promote the deputy chief. However, Ellis felt the community likely would not accept this and he was not sure if he could, either. As well, his appointment had to be confirmed

---

[1]The mayor had once accused the chief of taking time off and not charging his leave bank, which was ultimately not true.

by the city council and it is likely the four who would not make Deputy Chief Collins manager would not make him chief, either. After conferring with the council, Manager Ellis decided to conduct a national search for Grover's replacement. Advertisements were placed in two national police journals, and the applications flooded in. In all, over 200 applications were received by the city of Woodside from all over the country.

Ellis was told that there would have even been more had he not described the town as racially diverse. It seems every police officer has the goal of someday becoming a police chief. With that many applications, the manager faced a Herculean task indeed. About 150 were easily eliminated, including those from college students, clerical workers, laid-off auto workers, police chiefs in towns where they were the entire police department, and other applicants clearly not qualified. Ellis winnowed the fifty down to ten for interviews.

In his first foray into the hiring process for the police chief (he had hired clerks and maintenance workers), Ellis felt that it would be best to form a blue ribbon panel of experts and community activists to assist him with the process. This panel consisted of two council members, a vocal community activist who attended nearly every council meeting, the police chief of a neighboring community, a state police captain, a representative from the prosecutor's office, the city attorney, and two members representing local civic groups.

Several residents and activists in the community wanted the interviews to be open to the public. The local news media not only insisted on this but demanded it. City Manager Ellis, however, felt that in order for them to be frank and honest interviews, they should be closed. As it was simply an advisory panel, he did not consider it to be a public body and, thus, was not subject to the state's open meetings act. The city attorney concurred.

For the purpose of this case study, only three interviews are noteworthy. Deputy Chief Collins was, of course, a courtesy candidate. His interview was mostly matter of fact and the panel was not overwhelmingly impressed.

William Carson was a police chief from a similar community in another state. His interview was impressive. Somewhat quiet and mild mannered, he seemed to possess the tact and leadership needed for the position. The panel was satisfied with his interview but seemed only lukewarm to him.

The third and last candidate stormed into the interview room with his commanding 6-foot-4 square-framed presence, walking aggressively and with confidence. His name was Orson Cobb, and he was carrying his briefcase. He approached the front of the room and placed the briefcase on the panel's table in front of City Manager Ellis. As he opened the case, it blocked Ellis's view. Cobb reached into case and extracted a flashy gold badge larger than the size of a typical computer mouse. He handed the badge to the interviewer at the end of the table and asked the panel to pass it down to each other as he explained its significance. In a deep voice with a Boston-like accent, he said "Ladies and gentlemen, that badge was presented to me as a token of esteem and affection by the Hispanic and Black League of the precinct in South Chicago, where I was the captain for 8 years before my retirement." City

Manager Ellis's first notation on his pad was "door-to-door salesman." For the past 3 years, Cobb had served as police chief in a town in a different midwestern state. He said that he quit because the town council, whom he reported directly to, was corrupt.

The panel was particularly impressed with his interview, experience and qualifications. They were especially bowled over with what he would do if he caught an officer on the midnight shift sleeping in his patrol car. (Cobb had told the panel he would be out on patrol supervising the department day and night.) Cobb said that he would get out of his car, walk up to the patrol car, tip it on its side, "shake the cop out, and ask him, 'what in the hell do ya think you're doing?'"

The city manager was not impressed with Cobb. His choice was the second candidate, Carson. References provided by both candidates were checked and were glowing. Ellis could not quite put his finger on it but there was something about Orson Cobb that did not seem right. But Cobb had wooed the blue ribbon panel, and he was their unanimous choice.

Mr. Ellis was faced with quite a conundrum. Should he go with his gut or go with the flow? His gut told him that Carson was the best choice. But his hand-picked blue ribbon panel had unanimously chosen Cobb. How could he turn his back on them? He decided to go with the flow and appointed Cobb. The City Council confirmed his appointment by the now seemingly standard of a 4–3 vote. For a time, all was well.

Word reached the community where Cobb had been chief and the flood of media inquiries began. Was Ellis aware that Cobb was being sued by two female clerks for sexual harassment? Was Ellis aware that on more than one occasion Cobb was seen drinking on duty and that on more than one occasion he had returned from lunch to his chief's office intoxicated? Was Ellis aware that Cobb had been in an accident with his city vehicle in a section of a nearby central city frequented by prostitutes? Was he aware. . . ? Was he aware. . . ? Was he aware. . . ? Cobb, of course, denied all of the allegations, saying that they were rumors perpetrated by his corrupt town council and political enemies.

The local Woodside media, of course, entered into the frenzy. The city of Woodside, its new police chief, and its relatively new city manager were front page news for nearly 2 weeks with scandalous headlines. An editorial gave new Chief Cobb the benefit of the doubt and wished him well as Woodside's new police chief. But they chastised and scathed City Manager Ellis for the secrecy in the selection process.

Ellis's "gut" was correct. Chief Cobb was a disaster. He was the disappointment the city manager had feared. From the outset, Cobb alienated all but a handful of people both within and outside of the police department. He was not the round-the-clock chief that he had assured the blue ribbon panel he would be. He usually came into the department around 9:00 or 9:30 in the morning and was always gone by 5:00, even earlier on Fridays. He rarely went on the road as he promised he would. His management style was condescending and abrasive. His chain smoking (three to four packs a day) added to his negative persona.

Chief Cobb spent weeknights in a tiny apartment in Woodside and left every Friday to drive over 400 miles to spend the weekend with his wife. He told City Manager Ellis that he would not move to Woodside until he was given assurance that he would have a long tenure with the city. Ellis could not give him that assurance.

Cobb was Ellis's first chief hired, and his first chief fired. Cobb lasted 6 months.

Questions

1. Was the mayor unethical by being overly involved in the police department?
2. Did the city manager violate Tenet 11 of the ICMA code of ethics by politicizing the interview process with a blue ribbon panel?
3. Would it have been more ethical for the city manager to have had an open selection process rather than a closed one? Was this in violation of Tenet 9 of the ICMA code?
4. Was Chief Grover's resignation an illegal constructive termination because of his race?
5. What would be the likely community reaction if Ellis had trusted his gut and appointed William Carson?
6. How could Ellis have better handled this appointment? Did he fail to do an adequate background check on Cobb?
7. How should the manager have handled the racial overtones borne by the mayor?
8. What, if anything, should the manager have done to address the mayor's hands-on approach to his part-time job?
9. What action could the manager have taken to prevent the mayor and others in the police department from undermining the police chief?
10. Was the manager wrong in allowing the police chief to keep the city vehicle during his 2-month leave of absence?
11. Under the spirit of the Open Meetings Act, should the city manager have allowed the police chief interviews to be open to the public?

Chapter 4

Oh, the Tangled Web We Weave

"When I do good, I feel good; when I do bad, I feel bad. That's my religion."

—Abraham Lincoln

The local television station did a very flattering feature report on City Manager Bill Nelson. It showed footage of him umpiring Cannon Edge's Little League baseball games on a Saturday afternoon at the city's ball diamonds. In full regalia with his blue shirt, gray pants, black chest protector, and catcher's mask, Nelson told the reporter that he enjoyed his volunteer work with the league every Saturday during the summer months. He said that he first got interested in sports as a child, himself a Little League player in his younger years. He also played high school ball as a starting pitcher and was awarded a full scholarship to Central State College. He told the reporter, however, that his college baseball career was cut short due to a disabling arm injury. Had it not been for that injury, he had envisioned a career in major league baseball. He was that good, he stated.

Instead, he chose a career in local government management. He started out as a police officer in a small western Nevada community. Later he became its assistant city manager, then city manager. As is common in the city management field, he moved up to a much larger city, Cannon Edge, in a neighboring state. Not only was it a larger city, but it was also a growing city. With growth comes increased tax revenues, and the city had more money to spend than it knew what to do with. City Manager Nelson was at the helm of the city for nearly 18 years. During his tenure, the city hall underwent a multimillion-dollar renovation (including the repaving of the street to city hall and renaming it Nelson's Way), streets were paved, and water and sewer lines were installed. Two brand new, huge fire stations were built. Each fire station was equipped with the best firefighting equipment taxpayer money could buy.

Nelson was a member of the International City/County Management Association (ICMA) and active in the state's city management association, serving first on its board of directors and later as president. He was involved in the capital area chapter of the American Society for Public Administration (ASPA). He was a recipient of the chapter's Public Administrator of the Year award in 1998. He was a highly regarded professional city manager.

On his resumé and online biography, in addition to his experience, he boasted a bachelor's degree in business from Flushing College. He also cited another bachelor's degree and a master's degree in public administration from Monarch University.

Exactly how it came to light is uncertain, but a reporter from the *Cannon Edge Weekly* became suspicious of Nelson's educational claims. When confronted, Nelson readily agreed to fax his transcripts to the reporter. Something appeared out of order to the journalist. He contacted Flushing College and it had no record of Nelson ever having attended there, let alone graduating from there. The faxed transcripts were a forgery. Nelson had used another person's transcripts and superimposed his name on them. Further investigation found that Monarch University was an unaccredited online paper mill. For the right price, one could buy a degree in almost anything from Monarch U. His college baseball career at Central State was a hoax as well. The closest he came to ever stepping foot on that institution's campus was when he passed one of its satellite centers on his way to get his hair cut from time to time. A video from his initial interview for the city manager's position shows him stating, "I hold two bachelor's degrees and a master's degree in public administration." Eighteen years later he had to admit these were lies.

At a press conference, as tears rolled down his face, Nelson admitted that he had lied about his credentials, but he refused to step down. He cited his stellar career and long record of accomplishments in Cannon Edge. "It got to the point where I just started to believe it myself and for that I apologize," he said. "I intend to continue to serve the city as its manager. I meet the requirements and have the qualifications as required by the city charter," he added. The city charter required a bachelor's degree or 3 years experience as a city manager. As he had been with the city for nearly 18 years, he felt that he met this latter requisite. He implied that this "mistake" was made a long time ago and, as such, should be overlooked.

A political storm was swirling in Cannon Edge. While Nelson had his supporters, the detractors were quickly outnumbering them. Many were demanding that he immediately resign while others were calling for the city council to fire him. Among his supporters was the mayor. "After leading this city for 18 years, his record speaks for itself," the mayor told a local reporter.

A former fire chief, who Nelson had forced to retire a few years earlier, forcefully called for his immediate termination. "If you lied on your resumé that makes you a liar. And a liar should not be in charge of the city!" the former chief was quoted as saying.

The groundswell continued to mount with almost all residents following the story demanding the city council terminate Nelson. Because of this, the city council was really left with little choice. A long-serving council member choked with emotion introduced the resolution. "I move to terminate the employment contract between city manager William Nelson and the city of Cannon Edge immediately for falsifying his employment application." The city council voted reluctantly but unanimously to approve the resolution. Nelson left the council chambers without comment.

The city of Cannon Edge was not the only employer Bill Nelson had duped. About 2 years earlier, he had applied for a teaching post at Cannon Edge Community College; teaching is a common sideline for city managers. He listed his bogus degrees on his employment application with the community college. Impressed with his credentials, the college hired him as part of its adjunct faculty. And he taught a class. The class? None other than Ethics in Government!

After his termination, Bill hung his head a bit low and kept a low profile. Both the ICMA and the state city management association voted to ban Nelson from membership permanently. "It is essential that our members adhere to the highest standards of ethical conduct in order to maintain public confidence in their profession, their local government, and in the performance of the public trust," the state association's newsletter stated. It continued, "When an association member fails to abide by the code of ethics and brings discredit to the association and profession, then it is incumbent upon us to take appropriate disciplinary action."

Nelson tried a web-based consulting service believing (hoping) that other public managers locally, statewide, and perhaps even nationally would pay for his sage advice. The well-designed web page featured a smiling Nelson and his long list of accomplishments. Over 20 years in public management . . . balanced operating budgets in excess of $80 million . . . capital budgets and improvements ranging from $1 million to over $20 million . . . experienced in collective bargaining and labor relations. It did not say where and it did not say how. Nor did it list any educational background. He had few, if any, inquiries. But ex-city manager William Nelson did not have to hang his head low for long.

The *ex* would soon be removed from his title and he once again could hold his head high. In fact, it took less than 6 months for Nelson to rejoin the ranks of city management. The city of Fletcher Mills was in the market for its first city manager. Located about 40 miles west of Cannon Edge, but still in the same general metropolitan area, Fletcher Mills had a population of less than a fourth of Nelson's previous town. Also unlike the booming Cannon Edge, Fletcher Mills was an older community facing financial troubles. It had a deteriorating downtown and a declining industrial tax base. The mill from which it had derived its name closed more than a decade earlier. But nonetheless, its community leaders were optimistic, especially after deciding to have a professional city manager lead the city.

They were aware of Nelson's troubled past, but they did not view this as a deterrent, but rather as an opportunity. They unanimously voted to offer Nelson the job and he readily accepted it. "I have always enjoyed working in the public sector and am pleased to be able to do it again," a smiling Nelson told a local reporter. "It is the most fulfilling job you can have." While he took a significant pay cut, he was back in the proverbial saddle again.

"This is a man who's made mistakes in his past, admitted to them, and is looking to move on," the Fletcher Mills mayor said. "This will all be done to our city's benefit. Having a professional manager here day in and day out is important to Fletcher Mills's future."

Another council member chimed in, "This is a happy day for our city. Best move we have ever made."

Even a council member who said the city would be nuts to consider him jumped on the bandwagon. After listening to him at his interview she found him head and shoulders above the rest.

Another colleague concurred. "I believe opportunity has knocked on our door and this council has opened that door wide," he said. "Bill Nelson, arguably a star in the field of city management, has come to our doorstep." The local paper reported that Nelson had received numerous awards during his tenure with Cannon Edge, including the coveted Public Administrator of the Year from ASPA's capital area chapter.

Even a regular council critic supported the move, saying to the council "You're going down the right road. This will bring Fletcher Mills out of the Dark Ages. I think you have selected a good guy."

Although she voted for Nelson, Councilmember Wilma Donner expressed reservations over his ouster from both the ICMA and the state city management association. She commented that the city was at a disadvantage with its top executive unable to attend professional meetings and workshops and to network with other city managers.

The mayor disagreed. "I am more concerned with the skills and ability our city manager brings to the table as opposed to what social clubs he is a member of," the mayor stated. "We get plenty of information from other sources that allow us to stay up to date with the goings on that are of concern to our city."

Another council member concurred. "Bill Nelson is a talented public administrator, and input from an outside club holds no weight in my eyes. Membership in these associations does not reflect on his abilities one bit," he said. "Frankly, they are lesser organizations by not having Bill Nelson as a part of them."

Nelson hit the ground running in his first several months as Fletcher Mills's first city manager. A key priority on the city council's list of goals was to bring Fletcher Mills into the modern era by having a web site. Nelson set out not just to build one, but to build an award-winning one. Its home page contained a community description and municipal mission statement. It was brief—only four short paragraphs in all. When the site was launched, it was discovered, uncertain how, that two of the four paragraphs were strikingly similar . . . identical . . . to the home page of another city in a different part of the state. That city's web page was an award winning one.

At first, Nelson said that he did not know who had written the passages. When pressed, he said that he had authored them. "I do recall visiting sites that reported examples from award winning web pages," he said. "It now appears that two out of four paragraphs on the home page were influenced from the content of these examples available at that time." Thus, he only plagiarized two of the four paragraphs.

As of this writing, Nelson has served as city manager of Fletcher Mills for 2 years and continues to do so. In that capacity, he serves in leadership positions in the community and in an alliance of metropolitan communities.

Questions

1. Where does one even begin to evaluate Mr. Nelson's ethical lapses? Which of the twelve ICMA Code of Ethics tenets did he *not* violate?
2. Are city managers true professionals in the strictest sense of the word?
3. Is city management a profession akin to medicine, law, accounting, etc.?
4. Are the ICMA and its state affiliate a social club as one council member described them?
5. Did the ICMA and its state affiliate overreact by barring Nelson from membership? Would not a public censure be more appropriate? After all, the ICMA does not require it members to have college degrees.
6. Is there a strategy that Nelson might have successfully used to keep his position with Cannon Edge?
7. Does the nearly 18 years of city manager experience trump the fact that he held no college degrees?
8. Should the length of time elapsed since his application as Cannon Edge's city manager have been a factor in his firing?

Chapter 5

To Tell the Truth

"That you may retain your self respect, it is better to displease the people by doing what you know is right, than to temporarily please them by doing what is wrong."

—William J.H. Boetcker

Andy Sylvan was the assistant director of the community development department of the city of Greenwood. Greenwood was an outer suburb of the capital city, and while most of its citizens were affluent, it did have a pocket of residential poverty near a riverbank across from an urban industrial complex. Sylvan was active in writing grant proposals for both federal and state funding of a redevelopment project. One of his state grant applications was successful, and the state government awarded a block grant of $3 million for renovation of the area. The renovation money would permit the community development department to purchase land and build a park near the area's elementary school, to pave several streets, and to improve the storm drainage system. Money would also be available to bring plumbing systems in several homes up to code standards. Sylvan's boss, Rose Almindinger, was a political appointee who was well connected to leaders of the local Republican Party.

While she had had administrative experience with a construction firm, she had never been in charge of financial affairs in any sense beyond balancing her personal checkbook. One has to seriously question if she did that very well. What she seemed not to understand was that the moneys that came from state grants were not to be mixed with her private bank accounts. Almindinger was sort of like George Washington Plunkitt[1] in that she believed in honest graft, that is, when she saw her opportunity, she took it. The grant and its block structure sure looked like an opportunity. After all, just what is community development? Almindinger saw a chance to arrange bids for street construction so that her former company could win the business at a higher price than others would charge. A glaring loophole in the grant system seemed to suggest that she could award contracts without going through the city's purchasing and bidding systems. She also found leeway to attend a conference on park development in Hawaii on the state's dollar. A friend of hers ran a travel agency and she was more than anxious to help Rose. In fact, she told Almindinger that she could bill her for travel expenses for both her and her husband in a way that it would appear that all airline costs were for one person. The two enjoyed 7 days on Maui, all expenses paid by the city, while Mrs. Rose Almindinger made brief appearances at the 2-day conference. Almindinger also hired four political friends for temporary jobs on grant projects, paying them $40 an hour. No one managed the four, and only Almindinger received reports of their work. Their employment cost the grant $30,000 in just 2 months.

While there was evidence of some improvements being made in the grant project neighborhood, rumors of waste, fraud, and abuse started to circulate. One of Almindinger's appointees had a penchant to be verbally abusive to certain assistants in the department office, and the assistants had contacted the city personnel director. Sylvan heard about the abuses, and he talked with the employees. That's when he heard also about some of the financial problems in the project, and that's when he heard about Almindinger's trip to Hawaii with her husband. She had told Sylvan that she had to take a week of leave time to travel to North Carolina to be with her sick father.

While all of this was going on, Almindinger announced that she was going to be running for the state assembly. Her four project appointees soon were circulating petitions door to door and also around city hall gathering names so that she could be on the ballot. Sylvan sensed that there was a severe violation of the state's Little Hatch Act in this activity. Without warning to Sylvan, one day a reporter showed up at city hall and started asking questions about the grant project. Sylvan was very careful to avoid the reporter, once barely missing him by ducking into the men's room. He then snuck out a side door and phoned his assistant to tell him he was taking his lunch break early.

The reporter did not gather much information, but he did drop a few lines in his weekly local affairs column suggesting that the state might be looking into irregularities in grant programs at Greenwood city hall. Governor Tyler Phillipson was facing a tough reelection campaign. The Democrat was facing an even tougher fight

[1]See Riordan, William. *Plunkitt of Tammany Hall.* Boston: Bedford Books of St. Martin's Press, 1994.

to keep the state House of Representatives' majority with his party. The Greenwood seat was open, but it had been held by a Democrat. The district was considered very competitive, and the Democrats had not been successful in recruiting their first choice as a candidate. Douglas Springfellow, an Iraq War veteran, had expressed interest, but at the last moment he told Phillipson that he really had to get on with life and support his family by taking a management job with the local chemical company. The Democrats then found Professor Howard Hopper, a regular activist since the Vietnam War, to carry the party banner into the race. Governor Phillipson agreed to come to Greenwood and organize a fund raiser for Hopper, but he was sure that Almindinger's campaign would easily outspend the Democrat. When rumors of the grant problem hit the governor's desk it was like a godsend. With his authority and the help of the state attorney general, also a Democrat, they could expose Almindinger.

He needed some proof from someone close to the scene. He had his associates snoop around Greenwood to gather information. One name they kept coming up with, a name that was on all the grant applications, was Andrew George Sylvan.

Sylvan was sitting at home watching *Aaron Cooper 360* on CNN when his phone rang. The caller asked, "Hello, Andrew, how are you tonight?"

Sylvan was fearful it was a request for charity. He gave a meek, "Yeah, I'm O.K., what do you need?"

"Andrew, this is Tyler."

"Tyler who?"

"Tyler Phillipson—Governor Phillipson. Could we talk a minute?"

Andy was rather shocked. He had met the governor only once before and that was in a reception line at a capital chapter meeting of the American Society of Public Administration. He was sure the governor would not remember that.

But sure enough, the governor said, "Andrew, we met at, let me think, it was the meeting of that public administration group down at Celentinos on Chicago Street. When was that, oh, must have been 7 or 8 months ago."

"Boy, the governor's staff really does its homework well," thought Sylvan, but he said, "Well go ahead, what you need?"

The governor told Sylvan that the state was dedicated to the highest standards of ethical behavior by all its public employees at all levels, and the state was very desirous that taxpayer money always be spent in the most efficient manner. If the money on grant programs was spent efficiently, more grant money would be available for worthwhile projects. Soon he had Sylan talking, and soon the words flowed out of Sylvan's mouth. Sylvan had been in the municipal bureaucracy for over 20 years, and he, too, was dedicated, and right's right, and wrong's nowhere as far as he was concerned. He revealed what he knew, and in fact, he knew a lot. He also gave names and places and indicated where what he said could be verified. He simply spilled his guts.

Governor Phillipson offered his warmest appreciation for his help, and he told Sylvan to be sure to stop by when he got to the capitol the next time. Sylvan was also told that if he ever needed help on anything not to hesitate to call the governor's office. The governor called him a brave and treasured government employee. "We need more like you," the governor said.

The next week the city manager, Fred Gardner, send a short note to the staff of the department of community development. It simply said that Rose Almindinger had resigned to work full-time on her state legislative campaign, and that the assistant city manager, Franklin Millard, was going to be acting as the director of the department for the near future, until a replacement could be made. Also all professional staff of the department was being given a 1-week leave of absence without pay, during which time the state attorney general's staff would be conducting an audit of department expenses. Other staff were directed not to speak to anyone about the affairs of the department—especially the press.

Andrew Sylvan immediately made an appointment with the city manager. When he talked to him the next day, he found the manager to be quite distant to him, although he had been on friendly terms with Gardner for 3 years. He asked about the vacancy at the top of his department, indicating that he had been with the department for over 10 years and he had his M.P.A. degree. He suggested that he was quite familiar with the work and all the people in the department. Gardner simply told him that at this time it would not be wise for him to consider applying for the opening. He added that under the circumstances they would probably be going outside for a new director. Sylvan left the office quite unsettled. A few days later he saw Gardner at a popular restaurant in Greenwood and he approached him ready to shake his hand and say hello. The manager clearly saw him and turned away from him in an awkward manner as he approached. It was a very obvious rebuff. Sylvan, whose wife was with him, was hurt.

Three weeks later, the city manager publicly announced that an audit had found some normal accounting mistakes in the books of the community development department, but that the attorney general's report revealed no wrongdoing on the part of city staff.

Not only was Sylvan out of the loop for a promotion, but at the end of the year he received only a satisfactory evaluation. Every year before—for 20 years with the city—he had received either commendable or excellent ratings. He was also notified that he would not receive any merit pay, although over half of the staff did receive merit pay. Over the ensuing months since his discussion with the governor, Sylvan noticed that other employees around his department and at city hall seemed to avoid him. Even good friends would just say, "Hello" in passing. As the new year started, he decided he should look for a position in another department. He saw a lateral opening in public works, and he submitted a full application. Not only did he not get an interview, but his application did not even gain an acknowledgement.

Sylvan talked to a good friend at the community college, and he was given an opportunity to teach a class during the summer term. That went so well that he applied for and received a regular teaching appointment the following year. He had to take a substantial cut in pay, but his colleagues spoke to him, and his students especially liked his real life stories about how bureaucracy really worked.

Governor Phillipson was reelected to a second term, and afterwards accepted an appointment as a federal district judge. Rose Almindinger found that her campaign for the legislature was stymied as major funding sources she had counted upon dried up, and the press came out strongly in favor of Hopper, the winning candidate. Almindinger went back to work as a glorified administrative assistant with the state contractor's association.

Questions

1. Why did the governor allow Sylvan to be punished after he helped the governor "get the goods" on Almindinger?

2. Should Sylvan have remained quiet when he was called by the governor?

3. Should Sylvan have spoken to the city manager as soon as irregularities were obvious in the neighborhood grant program?

4. Would the city manager's response have been the same if Sylvan had taken the problems to him?

5. Were the governor and attorney general really concerned about wrongdoing in the community development department, or was the governor only seeking political advantages in his inquiries?

6. Should Sylvan have taken his situation to the local press? What would they have done with his story?

7. How do you suppose Judge Phillipson would rule if a whistle-blower case was brought to his bench?

Chapter 6

Dirty Job? Hire a New Person to Do It

"Sometimes the best way to say 'No' is to say 'Yes,' and then just not do it."

—**William Thompson**

Sewers can be dirty business, but then they add to the health and safety of communities. In 1972, the United States Congress appropriated funds for construction of sewers in rural communities of America. Eligibility depended on the density of the local population and whether the community already had sanitary sewers. The small north central community of Brooklyn was a likely candidate. However, residents in the community had invested money in septic tanks and their upkeep, so the political sell to have sewers would not be an easy one.

Fortune shined on the city fathers as Richard Nixon impounded funds for the project, claiming that the federal budget was too large and deficit spending was endangering the general economy. Nixon's action stood for several years. However, a lawsuit finally reached the U.S. Supreme Court, and the justices ruled that the president was without general authority to impound authorized funds for projects such as rural sewer construction. Funds were ordered to be released. A few more years passed before the state government was told that it would receive over a billion dollars for eligible local sewer projects. The citizens of Brooklyn were a bit more receptive to the idea this time, but opposition was still strong.

The state requested that eligible communities pass sewer construction ordinances and then apply to the state Environmental Protection Agency for the federal funds. The local governments would be given one half of the money needed to construct sewers. As the building of the sewers required tearing up streets, new street construction was also part of the project. The city would then have to issue bonds to cover the remaining cost of the project. The city of Brooklyn proposed that the costs of the bonds would be repaid through charges to residents who hooked up to the sewer lines. While residents could not be forced to hook up, they would be forever prohibited from installing new septic tanks.

The city council held hearings, and they took in an earful—mostly from residents who had just installed new tanks or who were convinced that tanks were every bit as good as those smelly sewers. If direct democracy was in effect, it is likely that the project would have lost a local vote. But local governments have representative democracy. The city council members were reasonable, and they listened to their engineering consultants and officials from the health department. Urbanized areas with sandy soils like Brooklyn had could not long subsist with only septic tanks. The end to this rural style of sanitation was coming near. The release of federal funds was a godsend, and the time to act was at hand. The state told the eligible local governments they had only 3 months to make their applications for funds. Under the leadership of Mayor Elliott Ferdon, the Brooklyn council voted unanimously to apply for the funds.

By the spring of 1978, the state had selected Brooklyn to receive $50 million as one half the cost of building a sewer system for 8,000 houses and business structures. The funded project included 55 miles of new pavement for almost all of the city's streets.

For all his hard labor on the project, Mayor Ferdon had only won opposition from local citizens, and in the fall he was defeated for reelection by Dick Houghton. Houghton had been a nonvocal supporter of the sewer project, but all he said in the campaign was "We have to move on from here," and, "We just have to make sure it is done in a way that is good for all the citizens." Coming to office, Houghton did not have to make the difficult choice of having or not having sewers. But there were a lot of difficult hurdles to jump before the sewers became a reality. The city hired consultants to provide engineering plans and to conduct bidding for construction, and it hired financial consultants to negotiate the sale of $50 million in bonds to match the federal grant. The city council also had to devise a plan to assign costs for hook-ups for each building structure using the sewers. Was it to be by individual housing unit, by street frontage, or by evaluation of the worth of property on tax rolls? It was a technical matter to be worked out in an atmosphere of zero-sum games where each decision made one resident a winner and another a loser.

While interest rates had been steadily climbing through 1979, toward the end of the year they dipped to less than 7% for municipal bonds, and the city was able to sell the bonds for somewhat less than expected. As it readied to bid out eight different construction grants, for eight geographical sectors of the city, fear struck again. Inflation was well into double digits, and petroleum products such as asphalt that was to be used for new streets were at all-time high prices. Good luck struck again. Local unemployment was severe and construction companies had idle capital equipment and work crews that were either laid off or about to be laid off. Bidding was competitive, and the costs of actual bids were below those anticipated. Sewers for Brooklyn were to become a reality.

As these events were unfolding, the city telephones began to constantly ring with questions about the project. High on the list of questions was, When is my neighborhood going to have its streets ripped up? Will I be able to drive home? How will we get out of the house? When do we have to pay for hook-ups? If the city gives us a loan for hook-up fees, what interest rate will we be paying? What if we are too poor to make payments for hook-ups? And on and on and on.

One day during this growing turmoil—which was beginning to wear on the clerical staff—Mayor Houghton read in the *League of Municipalities* magazine that a city in Minnesota had installed a sewer hotline during the construction of its new sewer lines. Houghton phoned the manager of that city and they had a long discussion. Houghton talked with the council members and they agreed to give him gas money and 2 days off if he would drive the 400 miles to the Minnesota community and gather details about the system. He came back enthused. As the local Comprehensive Employment Training Assistance (a federal program also known as C.E.T.A.) office was in a large city close to Brooklyn, Houghton made a visit there as well. C.E.T.A. staff indicated that they could find a person to act as the key telephone answering person for the sewer hotline. The city council agreed to set up the system and use a C.E.T.A. employee whose salary would be fully paid by the federal government.

The system was quite simple. C.E.T.A. sent out a young woman, Olivia Forest, who was enthusiastic about getting a job. She was personable and said she enjoyed answering phones and talking on the phone. She was selected to do the job. Her training involved a series of interviews with the city engineering consultants. She learned each of their names; she learned how to contact each of them at any hour needed. She met with each of the construction leaders of the companies that won bids to do work. She then developed a system of identifying each city street and cataloguing days when work would be done on the street. Before the work started she would develop handouts that the city building department would take to the front doors of houses and buildings. The handout would indicate the number of the sewer hotline and Olivia's name. Olivia also held weekly meetings with the engineers and teams from the construction companies. Olivia had a direct telephone number, but all calls coming into any city telephone regarding sewers were forwarded to her. For financial information such as billings, she was able to refer the calls to the treasurer's office if they involved more than basic information.

The system was a jewel. Everyone else on the city staff was relieved to be able to do their regular jobs without interference. A jewel of a dirty job had been given to Olivia Forest. It was a job that lasted 8 to 5 like the other staff jobs. However, it was a job that permitted few breaks other than for lunch and a quick restroom jaunt. The job was a total overload. It would have been a severe job for anyone, and for Olivia it was more.

She had not worked for many months; she was a single mother with obligations to get one kid back and forth to school and another to a babysitter. She did have extra government financial support for these duties, but the time pressures were horrendous. She went from the frying pan of the city office literally to the hot kitchen of home to make dinners for her children. Without complaining, she tried, and by all accounts she did a great job for the first month. Then came the recurring headaches and the occasional sick days. Then she was gone for a week. Then Mayor Houghton learned that Olivia had had a breakdown and was at the mental health ward of a large hospital in the next city.

The system was a flawed jewel. Houghton called back the city manager in Minnesota, and he said there was a bit of an overload on the person in charge of the phones. He had not told Houghton before, but now he informed Houghton that they rotated the job each 3 weeks. That way they had ready fill-ins in case of sick days and vacation days.

Houghton went back to the drawing board. He gathered all the clerical staff together and gave them a bit of basic training in the system. They agreed to pitch in as long as Houghton and the city clerk and treasurer personally took their turns on the phone. All agreed, and an 8-day rotation system—1 day at a time—was established. Olivia returned to the office relieved that she would be trained now to do other more mundane clerical tasks. After a month back she agreed to become part of a 9-day rotation on the sewer hotline.

Olivia was favored the next time the city had a vacancy for a regular position. She had been kept on beyond her C.E.T.A. timetable on a temporary basis. She became a permanent city employee.

Questions

1. Was what happened to Olivia inevitable?
2. Could Houghton have anticipated the problems Olivia would face?
3. Should staff members at the Minnesota city have been more forthcoming about the overload problem?
4. Would it have been more reasonable to have started the program with a regular staff member at Brooklyn city hall?
5. Is it ethical to dump the dirty job on the new person?
6. How might the job have been less trying for Olivia?
7. Was it appropriate for the city to give Olivia preference over all other applicants in hiring when a new vacancy arose?
8. Was permanently hiring Olivia a violation of Civil Service rules that state that jobs must be advertised and that a search for job candidates must be done?

Chapter 7

A Time for Action– A Time for Reflection

"Good people do not need laws to tell them to act responsibly, while bad people will find a way around the laws."

—Plato

In 1985, the city of Martin Woods was struck by a tornado. The state law prescribed that the city alarms warning about an impending tornado could not be sounded unless an actual funnel cloud had been witnessed by a law enforcement officer and that officer had made a report to the station sounding the alarm. Martin Woods police officer Bruce Fiegel served as a volunteer fireman with Martin Woods during his off-duty hours. Fiegel took both jobs seriously—extremely seriously.

At 4 PM, Fiegel was on duty as the volunteer in charge of the Prospect fire station. He looked at the sky. It was ominous, to say the least. It was turning an ugly black and the wind was screeching. Trees were turning, birds were falling from flight. It was enough for Bruce Fiegel. He searched out the safest corner of the building, and as he headed toward a secure location, he sounded the tornado alarm. He had not seen a funnel cloud, nor had he received reports of a sighting of a funnel cloud. Ten minutes later, the tornado ripped through Martin Woods, tearing roofs off 300 houses, completely destroying four churches and a dozen houses before it devastated the downtown section of the adjoining city of Martin Groves. Five people were killed.

It was almost a Yossarian moment right out of *Catch 22*. Should Office Fiegel have been reprimanded for his illegal action in haste of seeking out his personal safety? Or should he have been given an award? In the words of Joseph Heller, should it be a "black eye" for the city, or a "red feather?"[1] Mayor Howard Woodson had no doubts. In the wake of the disaster, there were local heroes and Bruce Fiegel was recognized as one of them. He gave the citizens of Martin Woods an extra 5, 6, or 7 minutes of warning. Most were able to get to shelter.

The irony of the story is this: one week volunteer fireman Bruce Fiegel was given an award by the city council for his quick decisive action in sounding the alarm before the tornado entered the city. Two weeks later he was fired as a police officer of the city. Decisive action is appropriate sometimes, but not all the time. Fiegel was an all-the-time action guy.

The police chief, Harmon Thomas, had received over 25 citizen complaints about officer Fiegel's conduct as a policeman. No other officer on the small force of 20 had received as many as five citizen complaints about his or her behavior. The chief was concerned that each day Fiegel was in uniform, he was an invitation for a major lawsuit against the city. Two straws broke the camel's back in the eyes of Thomas. A month before, Fiegel was patrolling the poor area of the city—River Woods. He noticed a car parked outside a convenience store that had suffered several armed robberies. There were four teenage boys in the car—all were African Americans. They certainly looked suspicious—to Fiegel. He reasoned that this could be a crime in progress. There was no time for a stakeout or for a call for backup. He pulled out his gun and slowly approached the car. Getting a jump on the young men, he ordered them out of the car and he had them line up with their hands on the car. He cuffed two of them as he phoned for assistance.

At gunpoint, the teenagers remained against their car as another city police car roared into the parking lot with lights flashing and sirens at full blast. As the second officer approached the car and scouted out the convenience store, the store door opened and the boys' mother came out with a bag of milk, bread, and other goodies. The assisting officer led the retreat, uncuffing the two youngsters and offering apologies and excuses and he urged Fiegel to leave the scene immediately. The assisting officer made a report of the incident, and the parties involved—victims—filed a formal complaint.

The week before the tornado, Fiegel's true desire to see safety on the streets came out with another blaze of action. He sensed that the driver of a car in front of his was not in complete control. After following the car for two blocks, he decided he had to pull it over. He found that the driver was intoxicated and also resistant to his orders

[1]Heller, Joseph. *Catch 22: A Novel.* New York: Simon and Schuster, 1961.

to get out of the car. Officer Fiegel physically pulled the man from the car by force and rather briskly slammed him against the car as he cuffed him. The man was cussing at the officer and Fiegel was in a posture of readiness to strike the man when another Martin Woods patrol car came onto the scene. The other officer asked Fiegel to uncuff the man, which he did. The other officer then asked Fiegel if he had been in hot pursuit of the driver. Fiegel said he had, and that he had noticed the man's erratic driving two blocks back. "Two blocks back?" asked the other officer. Fiegel confirmed the distance. The other officer informed him that the Martin Woods city boundary was six blocks back, and that the entire episode had happened in Martin Grove.

The second officer called a taxicab and asked the man if he would mind leaving his car parked on the street at the spot and take a taxi home. He asked the man if he could pay for the cab, and the man said he could. In amazement the drunken driver got in the taxi cab and left the scene, not realizing that the Martin Woods police department had made a very serious error, albeit one in the interest—to a degree—of public safety. The second officer on the scene reported the incident to the chief, and the city officials collectively held their breath waiting for the lawsuit to be filed. It never was.

The city attorney concurred that Fiegel's behavior was inappropriate for a police officer and constituted justification for his removal. The police union said it would represent him, but that it would not present any evidence contrary to that known by the chief.

The action by Fiegel during the time of the tornado did not mitigate his other actions. Yet it bought time for contemplation. In consultation with the mayor and city attorney, Police Chief Thomas came up with a recommendation that won support of the city council. Officer Fiegel was to be placed on unpaid leave of absence pending a certification by a state police-appointed psychiatrist that he had a temperament that could enable him to return to duty. Fiegel would be dismissed from the force if he refused the conditions of his suspension.

Fiegel refused to be examined by a state police psychiatrist, and he was permanently relieved of his duties as a police officer. He remained on the Prospect station volunteer fire department staff.

Questions

1. Were the city officials being hypocritical in giving Fiegel an award when they knew that it was likely he was going to be fired as a police officer?

2. Should the city have discovered Fiegel's inappropriate personality traits when he was recruited?

3. Should the city have discovered Fiegel's inappropriate personality traits when he was at the police academy?

4. What special training might Fiegel have been given to correct his bad behavior?

5. Should the city have informed the drunk driver that his detainment was illegal?

6. Is there any role for people like Fiegel in the work of a police department?

7. Should the police chief receive a reprimand for not stopping Fiegel's actions before they reached the point they did?

Chapter 8

A Deadly Deed

"Neither fire nor wind, birth nor death, can erase our good deeds."

—Buddha

It was about 10 to 11:00 PM on a warm July night in the town of Bradford. "Nine-one-one, what is your emergency?" Dispatcher Sue Marks answered with the customary question on the 911 line.

"This isn't really an emergency," the caller replied, "I just want to let the police know that my husband is wandering the neighborhood wearing nothing but shorts and flip-flops. Just thought they should know that."

Knowing the name and address from the 911 system screen and being familiar with the caller, the dispatcher confirmed by asking "That's at 4242 Culver. Is that correct, Carol?"

"Yes," the caller confirmed.

"O.K. I'll make them aware of that. Thank you," the dispatcher responded.

About 45 minutes later, a second 911 call was received from 4242 Culver. This time it was from a 12-year-old boy calling from his upstairs bedroom telling the dispatcher that his parents were arguing and fighting. Dispatcher Karen Miller fielded this call and immediately dispatched two Bradford patrol cars to the home. Upon arrival, the police found the rear screen door open and the boy's mother lying in a pool of her own blood at the foot of the basement stairs. Next to the body with numerous stab wounds laid a portable telephone. EMS was summoned and she was pronounced dead on arrival at St. Mary's Hospital and Trauma Center.

Ben Fields had been Bradford's city manager for a little over 3 months. Just prior to his appointment, the city had also promoted the public utilities foreman, Daryl Connor, to the position of director of public utilities. That promotion created a vacancy that trickled down to an entry-level utility worker's position. Several factors limited the city's ability to attract and hire from a large applicant pool. First and foremost, at the time the city had a strict residency rule. An applicant had to be a resident of the city in order to apply for a job with the city. The advertisement process for vacancies in city government was mostly word of mouth. While Bradford's population exceeded 20,000, 35% of its residents were senior citizens.

The city also had a strict civil service system for all hirings and promotions. All candidates had to take and pass a written test. Those who passed the written test were then subject to an oral interview process administered by a panel of three outsiders unfamiliar with the needs of the city. All of this was, by the design of a true civil service system, an objective way of hiring city workers. Little, if any, management or subjective judgment need be applied. The system was so strict that the Civil Service Commission once refused to disqualify an applicant for a full-time position just because he had been terminated from a part-time position with the city. He was terminated from a part-time janitorial position for poor work habits, tardiness, and absenteeism. When he applied for a full-time position, the Civil Service Commission, on a unanimous vote, ruled that his termination was not a cause to eliminate him from consideration for a full-time position. "It's not in the rules. . . . It's not in the rules. . . . And if it's not in the rules, we can't do it. That would be illegal," the commission's chairman pontificated at the time. Apparently managing a law office qualified him to render legal opinions. The fired part-timer was allowed to test for the utility worker's vacancy. He failed the exam.

The other nine applicants for the vacant utility worker's position did pass the written and oral examinations and a Civil Service hiring list was completed. Top on the list was Wayne Hingle. Director Connor called Hingle and invited him to come to the Department of Public Utilities (DPU) offices for an interview. Hingle, in his early 30s, arrived promptly for his interview and was dressed appropriately. He answered the director's routine questions reasonably well. He told Connor that he currently worked for a landscaping company on seasonal basis and was looking for a job with better pay and benefits as well as a place from which he could retire. He did not impress the director as to being overly bright, but after all, the job was manual labor. High intellect was not a job requirement. Hingle had passed the Civil Service exam so, therefore, he was qualified by definition. He was offered the job and accepted it.

His first years with the city were uneventful. He came to work on time every day, did his job, did not complain, and mostly got along well with his coworkers. He was, however, somewhat of a loner. Wayne had two young sons and was active with Bradford's Youth Hockey Association. If he was not coaching, he was a proud father watching his sons fight it out on the ice. He was an exceptionally talented woodworker and could build pretty much anything out of wood that the city might need.

After the first 2 years, however, he began to act somewhat strange. No one could quite put their finger on it but something was not right with him. He would stare off into space, and his eyes had a certain glaze to them. If he disagreed with someone he would not argue with them. He would just give them a cold, penetrating, steely glare. It would frighten some of even the more macho utility workers. But he came to work every day and did his job.

Some of the other utility workers expressed their concerns and fears over Hingle's bizarre behavior to Director Connor. He turned to City Manager Fields for direction. When asked by Fields if Hingle had threatened anyone or assaulted anyone, Connor replied, "No, not yet, but I am afraid of him, too." Fields told him to monitor the situation and keep him advised.

Wayne Hingle's first contact with the Bradford Police Department occurred about 18 months before his last contact with them. A report of shots fired was called in to the department's dispatch center. Officers arrived at his residence and knocked on the front door. Hingle answered the door in a somewhat disheveled state holding his shotgun at his side. He seemed to be in a daze and confused why the police were there. When asked what he was doing he replied, "Aw, just got some squirrels in the attic and was trying to get them by shooting through the ceiling." While this was a rather creative and innovative approach to rodent control, it was also illegal. He could not understand why he could not discharge a weapon in his own home. The officers explained that someone in the home including him could be injured. He still did not understand. He was charged with reckless discharge of a weapon. He pleaded no contest and was given probation.

About 3 months after the squirrel-killing attempt, police were once again called to Hingle's home. This time it was a domestic violence call. It turned out to be only a verbal argument and no arrest was made. This happened again a few weeks later.

As none of these incidences were work related, his employment with Bradford's department of public utilities continued. However, so did the concerns over his bizarre and erratic behavior.

Several weeks passed, and Hingle's wife called Director Connor to tell him that Wayne had been hospitalized with a diagnosis of paranoid schizophrenia. She requested that he be placed on sick leave, which he was. Connor approached City Manager Fields with this news. "I told you he was crazy, and now he has papers to prove it! We can't have this nut working here," he protested.

Fields told him, "Let's just take this one step at a time."

Hingle was hospitalized for 3 weeks and took an additional week of sick leave. During that week he stopped by the DPU and gave Director Connor a doctor's slip authorizing his return to work the following Monday. Connor wasted no time in charging into the city manager's office screaming, "He can't be serious! We don't really have to take him back, do we?"

Fields explained that the city did, in fact, have to return him to work. A mental illness cannot be treated any differently than a physical illness.

Hingle worked 3 more weeks with the city before he fatally stabbed his wife, Carol Hingle, 39, of 4242 Culver Street, on that warm July night in the town of Bradford. Within minutes after he stabbed his wife to death, Hingle was found wandering, dazed and covered with blood. He was arrested, booked, and lodged in the town jail.

As homicides were very rare in Bradford, some confusion surrounded the events in the days following. Carol Hingle's extremely distraught and irate sister, Audrey Cook, who only lived a few blocks away, screamed at the police. She said that they caused Carol's death by not picking Wayne up when Carol first called 911. The sister claimed that she was speaking on the telephone with her sister when the attack occurred. She said she could hear Wayne say over the telephone to Carol, "They let me go," implying the police let him go. She also claimed that just prior to the attack her sister told her on the phone that she called 911 and asked them to pick Wayne up. This was all later be proven to be untrue as it would have been impossible. If she was talking to her sister when the attack occurred, the 12-year-old son would have heard this when he picked up the upstairs extension. He received a dial tone and called 911. The portable phone found next to the body was shut off.

Bradford operated its own emergency medical service. An EMT who had responded to the call and knew the Hingles and the Cooks urged Cook to file suit against the city for negligence. He told her that the dispatchers that work the 911 office were all incompetent and did not know what they were doing. He told her that they should have dispatched police cars immediately when Carol Hingle first called.

At the police station, a detective was called in to question Wayne Hingle, and after a short while agreed that he probably stabbed Carol. The following day, as Wayne Hingle sat in his jail cell, City Manager Fields terminated Hingle's employment with the town of Bradford.

Some council members and others questioned and criticized Fields's swift action. They argued that a man is innocent until proven guilty. As such, Hingle should have been placed on some type of leave until his innocence or guilt was determined. The city manager, however, reasoned that there is guilt in the criminal sense and then there is guilt in the employment sense. Whether he was found guilty or not guilty in a court of law was irrelevant. The man killed his wife and the manager was not going to keep a known murderer on his town's payroll.

Hingle was tried and convicted of first-degree murder. On a technicality, his conviction was overturned. He then pleaded guilty to second-degree murder and is serving a 25-year-to-life term in state prison.

Questions

1. Knowing the history of violence at the address, should a police car have been immediately dispatched after the first 911 call in July?

2. When can a worker's bizarre behavior be cause for official reaction? Must it affect actual job performance? Even if other workers fear harm to themselves or coworkers?

3. Should calls about domestic violence and concerns about mental illness affect one's standing in the workplace?

4. Must a city respect a doctor's opinion about a worker even when it disagrees with the opinion? Are city officials absolved of responsibility if they simply follow a doctor's opinion?

5. Was it unethical for the EMT to urge someone to sue his employer city?

6. Was it unethical for the city manager to terminate Hingle's employment before he was found guilty in a court of law?

7. Should the city manager have terminated Hingle's employment upon learning that he had been diagnosed with paranoid schizophrenia?

Chapter 9

Punishments to Fit Crimes, But Keep It Quiet

"The cosmos is neither moral nor immoral; only people are. He who would move the world must first move himself."

—Edward Ericson

Marion Wallingford had moved up quickly in the Melrose city bureaucracy. Melrose was a growing suburban city in an upper Midwest state. Wallingford was in the final stages of work on her master's in public administration degree when she was made the acting personnel director. After completing her professional paper on the subject of absenteeism in the workplace, she was given her degree. A month later she was promoted to the position of personnel director for Melrose. Marion's husband, Henry, was a professor of education at Fair Oaks State College where Marion did her graduate work. He was bright and always looking for an opportunity to publish and receive accolades of his colleagues.

Marion's major professor talked with Henry at the party the public administration department held for its graduates. He mentioned that Marion's paper was a quality effort, and that with some work, he might be able to make it into an article for a good education journal. Henry took the words seriously. That summer Henry and Marion worked over her professional paper and integrated some references to existing education literature into the text, and they sent if off to the *Midwestern Review of Education*, a peer-reviewed academic publication. In the fall, the coauthored article was accepted for publication, and it appeared in the next summer's issue. Henry was able to put the publication on his annual report, and in accordance with Fair Oaks State College procedures it was judged to be meritorious, and Henry received a merit raise of $2,000 for his efforts. The money went into his base salary.

Dewey Frieze was a personnel officer with the Westminster County sheriff's department. He had been a colleague of Marion's in graduate school, and he had also received a master's degree in public administration. Frieze and Marion Wallingford had been in the same public personnel seminar, which had been conducted by Professor Onslow Geddes. Geddes was a hands-on professor who encouraged class participation and a lot of group work. He had students write individual papers, but before they were submitted, the papers were circulated among members of the class and openly discussed. Frieze had been a negotiator with the county on its contract with the sheriff deputies' union that semester. A major issue in bargaining was longevity pay and merit pay and how attendance records could affect the pay. Frieze decided to dig into the topic, and he used his class term paper assignment as an opportunity to explore dimensions of absenteeism in public sector employment. He wrote his paper for Professor Geddes's class on this topic.

Two years passed by and it was time for contract negotiations again in Westminster County. Frieze was once again asked to be on the contract negotiations committee. In the 2 years of the existing contract, there had been several disputes and even a formal grievance over merit pay and the issue of absenteeism was central in one of the conflicts. The policy seemed to require further examination. Frieze, who was then teaching personnel courses at Westminster Community College, again decided to make a trip to the library and explore the literature on the topic. He did not find any article in *Public Administration Review* or in any municipal affairs journal that spoke to the topic, but there was an interesting title on an article in the *Midwestern Review of Education*. He was intrigued as he made his way down the bookshelf aisles of the Fair Oaks State College Library. The title sounded like it was right on the mark for what he needed.

When he opened the journal he was drawn to the text of the article. His first thoughts were that he must have read the article before. Maybe he read it when he was doing his research for that term paper for Professor Geddes. But no! The journal was dated a full year and a half after he had taken Onslow Geddes's class! But the words were just too familiar. Then it hit him. He exclaimed out loud, "My God! These are my words." He was reading parts of his term paper—word for word. He looked through the footnotes. To be true, several were for works he did not recognize, but most were sources he had used in his paper. He was stunned. Then he looked at the title again and under the title were the authors' names and their affiliations: Henry Wallingford, PhD, Professor of Education, Fair Oaks State College; Marion Wallingford, Director of Personnel, City of Melrose. Marion had stolen his work and passed it off as her own. He closely looked over all the references again, and he looked through the text line by line. Marion and Henry Wallingford had not given him the slightest reference or recognition as a person who had furnished material for the article. It was theft, and Frieze had caught them.

Frieze was a pretty easy going guy, but he was also ambitious, and he knew that a major publication like this article could be helpful in a career. He was angry. He knew he had to do something, but he also knew that he had to move carefully. Before he said anything he had to have his ducks in order. Fortunately, he occasionally had dinner and drinks at a local restaurant called the Gables on Friday evenings, and so, too, did Onslow Geddes. He bided his time, and 3 weeks later Geddes walked in alone just after Frieze had arrived. He invited the professor to sit with him in a corner and share a few drinks. Two drinks down each, he asked if the professor kept old term papers. "Meticulously, I do, I do." He asked if he could stop by his office and if they could both look at his paper from the personnel seminar. Geddes was a bit suspicious, but he agreed to do so that Saturday before the big game. The next day, they sat together as the article was retrieved from the file cabinet, and Frieze asked Geddes to immediately date it and sign on it that they were there, and to make a photocopy of it. He did so. Geddes told Frieze he could go one better. Geddes kept comments on copies of all the papers that had been circulated around the class—and he kept those papers, too. They were in a file that he rarely opened. But open it he did, and there the papers were—sixteen copies of Frieze's paper and the copy that Marion had taken home with her, along with her handwritten comments on it. This was proof it was Frieze's paper and proof that Marion Wallingford had taken it home and read it. Frieze made a copy but asked Geddes to keep the originals in a safe place. Then he confided to Professor Geddes what he had discovered.

Geddes was very hurt. To his knowledge, this had never happened in one of his classes before. He apologized that he had not been at Marion's paper defense, as he had left the campus early that May to go to Europe. But that was not more important a use of his time than sitting on Wallingford's review committee could have been. He could have stopped her and asked her to take the paper back and rewrite it before it was formally submitted. He was sure she would have done so if she knew that he was aware of what was going on. Then Geddes said, "Oh, my God, I could have stopped it then, and Henry would not have gotten involved. Oh, my God. I just had to take that trip."

Frieze told him that in no way should he feel guilty, that he had earned the trip. But Geddes told him, "Dewey, Henry is my friend—for 15 years he has been my friend." Geddes asked that Frieze make copies of the evidence and take the evidence to the dean of the graduate school, and that he do so without telling anyone else. Something would have to be done about the situation.

Frieze followed Geddes's advice, except that he also took the evidence to Devonshire Toumey, the city manager. The chairman of public administration, Rick Woodlawn, received a call from the provost, and he was asked to bring all of Marion Wallingford's records and papers to his office. The provost expressed dismay that someone from a newspaper had called a professor about a plagiarism case involving Wallingford. Woodlawn left the records with the provost. The provost told Woodlawn that he should immediately tell each of his faculty members that there would be severe disciplinary action taken if anyone spoke to a member of the press about the situation. Later that week the provost, graduate dean, dean of the college of education, and Woodlawn met with university attorneys and an attorney retained by Henry and Marion Wallingford.

Three days later, the *Melrose Citizen Patriot* reported that city personnel director Marion Wallingford had had her MPA degree taken away from her for violation of Fair Oaks State College procedures. City Manager Toomey indicated that the action did not affect Wallingford's employment, as the MPA degree was not really a job requirement, and besides she had a master's degree in philosophy anyway, so the second master's was really superfluous. He declined comment when asked if the case involved plagiarism, and he further declined comment when asked if Mrs. Wallingford was not the chairperson of the city's ethical practices committee. The newspaper indicated that no action was being taken against a professor who was involved with Mrs. Wallingford in publishing an academic article that seemed to be at the center of the situation. In fact, the provost had made an agreement with Professor Wallingford that he would return the $2,000 salary increase he had received. In return, the university would permanently seal the record of the case and the university would instruct all university community members that they could never speak about the situation again.

The *Midwestern Review of Education* was never contacted. Dewey Frieze was told no more about the situation than was in the paper. A month later he saw Professor Onslow Geddes at the Gables. Geddes said, "Come over, the drinks are on me tonight. Let's tie one on." Dewey smiled, and Geddes smiled back and shrugged his shoulders.

Marion held on to her job for 5 more years through the administration of the city manager and his successor. Her husband completed 30 years at Fair Oaks State and retired. The two then moved to San Clemente Island, California.

Questions

1. Did the punishment in this case fit the crime? Should either of the Wallingfords have lost a job?

2. Could Professor Henry Wallingford have acted in good faith in helping his wife publish the article? Should his name have appeared first on the article?

3. Why was the state college so adamant about keeping the matter out of the press?

4. Could the college have disciplined a professor for disclosing information to the press about the situation?

5. Did Professor Geddes have any obligation to become directly involved in the case?

6. Should the college have informed the *Midwestern Review of Education* that some corrections were necessary? Is it fair that all future readers of the article in the *Review* will think that it was written by the Wallingfords?

7. Was the university obligated to make any amends to Dewey Frieze? What could have been done for him?

8. If the situation is kept quiet, can the case have any instruction value for students and professors regarding their conduct in the future?

9. Was the city manager correct in saying that Marion Wallingford's behavior at the university was unrelated to her job?

Chapter 10

Boss, We've Got a Problem

"It is easier to sleep at night with a bad legal decision rather than toss and turn over a bad moral decision. In other words, 'Just go ahead and sue me.'"

—James E. Leidlein

Charlie Upton was viewed and admired as a professional policeman. He was well liked by everyone on the force. He headed the department's Child Protective Services, which essentially consisted of just him. He was mostly plain clothed, only wearing a uniform on occasion. Any matters involving juveniles called for Upton's intervention. Upton, a 17-year veteran of the police department, was born and raised in Summit, a mid-sized village in the Northeast. Like many communities, it seemed that everyone knew everybody, particularly the homegrown residents. Upton was one of these. He attended elementary and middle school and graduated from Summit High School. The high school principal, Mark Hammond, later became president of the Summit village council and he had regular contact with his former student, Upton. They had a close working relationship that became even closer when Upton ran for the Summit school board and easily won the election. The extent of Upton's popularity was further demonstrated when his fellow school board members chose him as their chairman.

Upton's involvement went beyond the village and the school district. Although not married or having any children of his own, he was heavily involved in youth activities, most notably his role with Summit's vibrant pee-wee football league. Pee-wee football, for boys ages 11 through 13, was a popular fall family activity in the close-knit town. Hundreds gathered on Saturday afternoons to watch and cheer for their favorite team. Upton was as much involved in this as he was in his job and the schools. He was on the league's board of directors, and in yet another example of the fondness Summit's residents held for Upton, the board elected him their president. Upton, of course, had his own team of twenty 11-, 12-, and 13-year-old boys. In fact, the village administrator's, own son, Timmy, was the star quarterback for Upton's beloved Raiders.

Competition was tough and sometimes brutal in the league, as the managers and coaches took the game very seriously. Winning was not anything—it was everything. This was especially so for Upton. His boys could not lose. It was not uncommon for him to be ejected from a game for arguing with a referee over a questionable call. Once, after a rare loss by his Raiders, Upton sat on the bench sulking while the boys from both teams reunited for their treats with the teams' mothers. Upton remained there by himself for well over an hour.

Nonetheless, everyone still loved him. They admired his devotion to his team, to his job, and to his school board work. After one fall football season, Upton stopped Village Administrator Tim Bell during one of his daily visits to the village hall. He told Bell that during the Christmas break he was planning to take the boys to his condo near Disney World as a reward for their winning season. He would treat all of them to a day at one of America's most popular theme parks. Upton thought Bell would be thrilled that his son would get a free trip to Florida. Bell wasn't. He told Upton that he did not think that was such a great idea. As it worked out, Upton dropped his plans to the disappointment of other residents who thought that this was just another gesture of Upton's generosity and good nature. The revelation soon to come out would split Summit wide open.

Another favorite season for Charlie was Christmas. Being rather robust, he filled the village's Santa suit rather well and made for a very believable Santa Claus. He loved to visit the Village's elementary schools as Santa around the holiday. He enjoyed nothing more than hoisting the little children onto his lap so they could tell him what they wanted for Christmas. He would tell them all to be good little boys and girls. The highlight of the season was when Charlie/Santa was delivered to the citywide Christmas party by helicopter.

Charles Upton held a secret . . . a very deep, dark secret. Charlie Upton was a pedophile. He liked and preyed upon little boys.

As was typical for Tim Bell, the telephone was already ringing in his village administrator's office when he walked in on a Monday morning. As expected, it was one of his council members in what most likely would be a long-winded conversation. They almost always were. His council was a demanding lot. They all wanted nearly daily updates on village business, particularly personnel matters. It was not unusual for Bell to spend 3 to 4 hours a day on the telephone with his elected supervisors. It did not appear that this day was going to be any different.

About 15 minutes into his conversation, Police Chief Martin Owens appeared at Bell's open office door. He looked flushed and something was obviously disturbing him as he stood at the administrator's door. Bell shrugged his shoulders indicating he did not know how long he would be on the phone. While Owens was used to this, he expected Bell's attention as he felt that his problem was more urgent than the gossip of a council member. Bell paced for 15 minutes outside the administrator's office, giving up in frustration by motioning to Bell to call him and mouthing the word, "Urgent."

By the time he finished the near hour-long telephone conversation with the council member, another one was on hold that took another 45 minutes. It was nearly 2 hours before Village Administrator Bell walked across the parking lot to the police department and into Chief Owens's office. By now, Owens was nearly beside himself and appeared quite worried and distraught. Bell sat in a chair facing the chief's desk while Owens, in what was highly unusual, closed the office door. As he sat down, Owens leaned forward across his desk towards Bell and said, "Boss, we've got a problem."

The chief related that he had received a telephone call first thing that morning from a social worker who was treating a 12-year-old boy for emotional problems. The provider told Chief Owens that the boy said he had been sexually molested by none other than the department's beloved Charlie Upton. When asked how reliable this source was, Chief Owens replied, "Very." The village administrator was also shocked and alarmingly commented on how Upton was his own son's football coach. Both the administrator and the chief agreed that this matter needed to be fully investigated and it should be done so by an outside agency. But what to do with Officer Upton while it was being investigated became a topic of heated discussion. Administrator Bell took the position that Upton should be immediately relieved of duty pending the outcome of the investigation. Chief Owens, already under community criticism for his strict disciplinary policies, wanted to place the popular Upton at a desk job until the allegations were proven or unproven. Upton's captain, his immediate supervisor, sided with the police chief.

All agreed, however, that the first order of business would be to call Upton in and confront him with the allegations. If he denied them, which all expected him to do, then Village Administrator Bell agreed to let the Chief assign Upton to desk duty. It was Upton's day off but the chief contacted him and told him to report to his office at 3:00 that afternoon. City Administrator Bell told Chief Owens to report to his office immediately following his meeting with Officer Upton. The meeting at 3:00 was a brief one, and the chief did as he was instructed.

When asked by the village administrator how Upton reacted to the allegations, Chief Owens said Upton stared at the floor for moments, then shook his head saying, "Well, there goes 17 years of police work down the drain."

The village administrator immediately took this as an admission of guilt and directed that he be immediately placed on unpaid leave and that he surrender his badge and weapon.

The outside agency advised that it would take 3 weeks to complete its investigation into the allegations. In the interim, only the city administrator, police chief, and captain were to know what Upton was being investigated for. No other city employees or city officials, including the village president and council, were to know.

During the investigative period, Chief Owens and Village Administrator Bell discussed at length how to deal with the media if charges were filed and the issue became public. They knew that there would be a media frenzy. A man with Upton's background and popularity being charged with child molestation would surely make good copy. Both Owens and Bell drafted anticipated media questions and even rehearsed their responses.

The investigation was completed and Upton was charged with criminal sexual conduct with a minor. He was immediately terminated. Before the charges were announced, Village Administrator Bell called a meeting of the village's department heads. To say they were shocked and in disbelief would be an understatement. No one said a word. Immediately following this meeting, the village administrator held a closed door session with the village council to advise them of the pending announcement that the village's police officer in charge of youth offenses was himself being charged with child molestation.

That meeting did not go well. The council was very vocal and upset that they were only just then being made aware of the situation. Three of the seven council members chastised the village administrator for his knee-jerk reaction. They argued that Bell shouldn't have terminated Upton when he had not yet been convicted. These were only charges, they said, that might not be true. They directed Bell to put Upton back in uniform and in a patrol car because even if he were guilty, which they did not believe he was, they believed he would never do it again. The village administrator refused to do so. He found it incredulous that council members would even think of putting a suspected child molester in a village police car.

The public announcement was made, and, as suspected, the town went into an uproar, with many residents coming to good ole' Upton's defense. The press descended en masse on Summit. In press interviews, his supporters all said essentially that the kid was lying. Charlie would never do that, they stated emphatically. A local television station reporter interviewed both Chief Owens and Village Administrator Bell. The news anchor, after seeing the field report, commented on the shock and disbelief on the faces of these two gentlemen "having just learned of these shocking charges." Both Owens and Bell, of course, had known about them for weeks. Apparently the rehearsals paid off.

A local television reporter confronted the superintendent of schools and asked what the school board planned to do while its president faced these charges. "We have determined that the victim was not enrolled in this school district and, therefore, it is not a concern of ours," was the superintendent's on-camera response.

Following Upton's termination, the village's finance director brought to Administrator Bell a separation pay form to sign. Traditionally (and contractually) employees who separate their employment are paid for their unused sick and vacation time. During his 17 years, Upton had accumulated about $26,000 in unused time. The administrator refused to sign it.

"I am not rewarding a child molester with $26,000," he told the finance director rather emphatically.

She argued that it was in Upton's labor contract, and, therefore, the village must pay it. She adamantly insisted that the Administrator approve the payment. He just as adamantly refused.

"Well, he is going to sue us," she said.

"Well, let him!" Bell disgustedly responded, "Let some judge order me to do it!"

Upton never received his separation pay.

Upton was arraigned and given personal bond with the condition that he have no contact with children. He hired an attorney and 2 weeks after his arrest he pleaded no contest to the charge. While this was not an admission of guilt, it is treated the same as if it were. He was sentenced to a year wearing an electronic tether and 2 years on probation. He served no jail time. To this day, some residents believe he was framed by the police chief and village administrator because they were jealous of his popularity and supposedly feared he had too much power in the community.

Questions

1. Was it unethical for the village administrator to pronounce Upton guilty based on his response when confronted with the allegation?

2. Should the village administrator have informed the village council as soon as he became aware of the allegation?

3. Was it appropriate for the administrator to be involved or should this just have been left to the police chief, especially in light of the fact that Upton was his son's football coach?

4. Was it ethical for the village administrator and police chief to rehearse their answers to the news media?

5. Was the school superintendent's response appropriate?

6. Was it unethical for the village administrator to refuse to pay Upton for his accumulated sick and vacation time?

7. Was the village administrator's refusal to reinstate Upton as directed by three council members unethical? Would your answer be different if a majority of them directed him to do so?

Chapter 11

Sometimes It's Tough to Explain

"To care for anyone else enough to make their problems one's own, is ever the beginning of one's real ethical development."

—Felix Adler

Sal Williams, the evening anchor of WNEW–TV, the major network affiliate in Wallingford, stuffed the microphone right into Mayor Peter Brockman's face. "Isn't it true that Officer Wells was in a traffic accident while on duty as one of your policemen?"

"Yes, sir," the mayor responded.

"And now you are trying to fire him because of his disabilities."

"That's a simple conclusion for a complicated case, sir."

"Well, it sure sounds that way to us, and I am Sal Williams, reporting from outside the chambers of Wallingford city council."

Sometimes things happen that take more than a sound bite to describe. Such was the case of Officer Jerry Wells of the Wallingford police department. Everyone in Wallingford liked Jerry Wells, and they certainly sympathized with him after his onduty traffic accident. The traffic report clearly revealed that another car ran a red light and broadsided Wells's police vehicle. After the wreck, Wells remained on sick leave at full pay for nearly 3 months. He had broken his leg in two places, and two vertebrae in his back had been chipped. Then he came back to light duty and finally to full duty. It appeared that he was fully recovered from the accident, and he was performing full duties as a police officer.

Wells loved sports, and he was always an available party to join a pick-up game of basketball, touch football, or softball. He had been warned by his doctors not to unduly exert himself over the next 6 months, although he was ruled fit for duty as a policeman.

During a pick-up game of basketball he tried to dribble behind his back and he twisted his leg and fell to the ground. He couldn't get up. An ambulance had to be called, and he was off to another long stay in the hospital. Again the city put him on sick leave. He left the hospital and went home to convalesce, and his available sick leave ended. The city put him back on the payroll with the understanding that he would return to work as soon as the doctors said he could.

Two months went by. Mayor Brockman was informed of the situation, and he talked it over with Police Chief Fred Arlington and with the city's personnel director, Jack Vinewood. All agreed that the situation could not persist this way forever. Either Wells would come back to work, or he would have to be removed from the force. The union representative of the police force indicated that the union would take action if he were removed from the force.

Finally, an ultimatum was given. Report to work or get fired. Wells came into work and requested that he be given a desk job. While his salary was two times that of a dispatcher, the police chief agreed to train him as a dispatcher. This took 2 weeks. Then Wells began duty on the police radio channels. The trouble was that his injuries required that he stand up every 20 minutes. The dispatchers were given 5-minute breaks every 2 hours. The city tried; the police chief tried; but Wells just couldn't sit still. He requested another desk job. There was no other desk job available. Wells then requested that he be made the city process server. This was a police position that was filled by a senior officer in recognition both of seniority and longevity, but also in recognition that an older officer could best handle the people-to-people contact of process serving and that the job was less demanding physically. The city needed only one process server, and the police department was not going to bump the incumbent holder of the position for Wells.

A second ultimatum was given. Show up for work as a patrolman or be fired from the force. Wells showed up ready to go to work driving a patrol car. However, he showed up with a walking cane. The chief sent him home. Wells was issued a final ultimatum: show up ready for patrol duty or you are done. Wells refused to show up.

Police Chief Arlington discussed the matter with personnel officer Vinewood, and they decided that the full city council would have to make a ruling on whether to keep Wells on the force in his nonworking capacity or to fire him. They recommended firing him. It was their position that taking no action just burned up city resources. All that time, Wells was being paid full salary. If he were fired, the city would have to pay no more salary. The union could complain, but it really could not take action, other than providing representation for Wells. Moreover, Wells could not take action against the city for disability pay and workmen's compensation until he was fired. The two decided that it was in Wells's best interest to be fired.

Mayor Brockman concurred, and he told the council that their vote would not be a vote against Wells, but rather a vote to resolve the case with some finality. The mayor also indicated to the council that his discussions with the city attorney convinced him that they had a strong case for avoiding a major disability claim as they had ample evidence that Wells was performing the full duties of his office at the time of his second injury, and that the second injury occurred while he was off duty and involved in an activity he had been warned about—exerting himself while playing basketball.

The city council went along with the recommendations and fired Wells. Sal Williams reported the action on the evening news in a way that was anything but flattering to the city.

Questions

1. Was the city obligated to fit Wells back into the workforce of the police department?
2. Should the police chief have given Wells the position of process server, as it was a duty he probably could have performed?
3. Should the city have fired Wells immediately after he had expended his sick time following the second accident—given that he was not able to report back to work?
4. Was the news media obligated to give the story more complete coverage, in effect presenting both sides?
5. Should the city have found a nonpolice job for Wells?

Chapter 12

Building Inspector: Too Good to Be True

"A man's ethical behavior should be based effectively on sympathy, education, and social ties; no religious basis is necessary. Man would indeed be in a poor way if he had to be restrained by fear of punishment and hope of reward after death."

—Albert Einstein

Mayor Fred Tappan was optimistic and upbeat on the January day when he was sworn in as the leader of the small Midwestern city of Shadford. But on the second day, a serious problem confronted him.

The city's young fire marshal, Bob Slauson, knocked on his door and said, "Excuse me, sir. May I have a moment?"

"Of course, Bob, good to meet you again. Come on in," the mayor said.

Slauson asked if he could close the door. Tappan agreed. Slauson then informed the mayor about a recent fire at an apartment complex in the city. Tappan had heard rumors, but he was about to get the facts. Slauson told him that the fire had started accidentally in a kitchen in an upper floor apartment at the end of the building. The fire moved into the ceiling and then the attic area above, where it should have been contained. The attic had fire walls between groups of units. Unfortunately, a hole had been cut into the fire wall. The fire spread across the attic area and moved downward into each apartment unit before fire personnel received a call and reached the blaze. It was daytime and almost all the residents were at work, so the call came late. The entire building was destroyed, but fortunately no one was hurt.

The building, like many others in the area, had recently undergone retrofitting for air conditioning. The company installing the air conditioning units cut holes in the fire walls in order to place air ducts to carry cool air from a central unit. The fire marshal showed Tappan the building inspector's report on the construction job. The report very clearly indicated that the holes in the fire wall had been filled in and the wall was fully capable of stopping movement of a major fire. To Tappan it was quite obvious that the building inspector had not physically inspected the construction job, or he was a liar. Tappan doubted the latter. Slauson concurred that it was a case of nonfeasance rather than malfeasance.

Slauson added that Bob Eberbach, the building inspector, was 66 years old, that he had suffered two heart attacks, and that he was not comfortable climbing up tall ladders. Climbing to high places is a basic job requirement for building inspectors. The city's failure had directly resulted in a major fire resulting in property damage exceeding a million dollars. The damage was covered by insurance, but if the facts were generally known, the city could have been liable in a lawsuit that would certainly have resulted in a major increase of insurance premiums paid by the city.

Tappan and Slauson agreed that their focus should be on the future, although each was queasy about not revealing the circumstances of the fire publicly. They confided with each other that they would not hide the truth if an outside inquiry was made. At that point the chips would fall as they may. Their concern, however, was what to do about Eberbach. Put another way, how were they to get rid of the building inspector?

Tappan quietly approached the city clerk, who was on the city commission, as was Tappan, and asked about the inspector's reputation. The clerk indicated that Eberbach was well loved, especially by the building community—that could be easily explained. The clerk added that the inspector had been with the city for over 30 years, and while he was physically slow and lacked energy, he was quite loyal to the city. Other city commissioners backed up the feeling that the inspector was a good employee. Tappan realized that a direct confrontation leading to a removal from office was not the best approach, from a political standpoint, for removing the inspector. He shared this view with Slauson, who agreed that the commissioners, especially the one who was a builder, liked Eberbach. He told Tappan he would think it over. Tappan, in the meantime, initiated a get-acquainted coffee meeting with Eberbach, where he very gently brought up the notion of retirement, asking Eberbach to tell him about the nature of the city's retirement system. The building inspector did so, but he added that retirement was certainly not in his plans, not at the moment anyway. Tappan dropped that part of the discussion.

A few days later, Slauson returned to Tappan's office. He said he had a strategy and he would like to get Tappan's approval. Tappan agreed. The fire marshal informed Eberbach that he was going to be following the building inspector as he did his rounds of inspections each day. He was going to get Eberbach's reports, and Slauson was going to check to make sure every point made in the reports was accurate, and that the reports were thorough. He told the inspector that he would be doing this for as long as it took to be assured that the Eberbach was doing his job fully and competently.

It only took 2 weeks. In late January, Eberbach came to Tappan's office, and he said that their previous conversation had got him thinking about retirement. Indeed, he had gone to the city treasurer, and he had found out that his retirement salary with Social Security was over 90% of his salary. "Why, you know I am working full time and doing all this stuff for only 10% more than that. It just doesn't make sense. I'm thinking, maybe it's time to think about me." Tappan suggested that he would be missed, and that the city certainly appreciated the long years he had given to his job. Eberbach, said, "Now don't try to talk me out of it. I'm giving my notice." Tappan and Eberbach both smiled, and laughed, and shook hands.

Tappan said, "You're not going without a party." They then agreed to a last date of work and a time for the good-bye party.

After the conversation, Tappan immediately phoned the state senator for their county. The senator agreed to get a resolution passed by the senate the next week. The resolution of praise was ready for presentation at the party. The cake had thirty-one candles, one for each year Eberbach had been with the city. Inside, Tappan felt a cringe of hypocrisy give way to genuine feeling of thankfulness for Eberbach's service as he noted a tear in Eberbach's eye during several tributes.

Tappan felt that by doing it right, the city was assured that Eberbach would not be coming back.

Next, Tappan had a major problem: who would the city select to be the next building inspector?

Tappan discussed the matter with Slauson and each of the city commissioners. A consensus developed that the city needed an energetic inspector who would make the builders toe the line. Even the builder on the commission agreed that the new guy should be ready to kick butt. The job was advertised in the state municipal affairs journal, and on the pages of newspapers in twelve major cities of the state. Soon the city had a small pile of applications. The commissioners agreed that Tappan, the clerk, and one of the commissioners would start interviewing. Ten candidates who lived within 20 miles of the city were called first. A marathon session lasting an entire day left the three basically exhausted and, to be frank, rather upset. No candidate seemed appropriate. One applicant was the father of the fire chief. He had been in housing construction. But he had not passed either the electrical or the plumbing exams mandated by the state. He had passed the construction materials exam and he had assured the board that he was going to schedule the other examinations soon. The other applicants also were deficient. One had failed the electrical examination three times, but he was confident that he would pass it next time. He assured the board that it was one "hell of a test." Others had passed the electrical test but had failed the plumbing test. A couple had no experience at all in building. Only one had worked as an assistant building inspector. Several had dropped names of friends that had various connections to the city. And so it went all day long.

It was time to look at the out-of-town applicants. One looked promising on paper, so he was invited to make a 200-mile trip from Morton, a city across the state. John Angell's record showed that he had over 20 years experience as an internal building inspector for a large manufacturing firm in Morton. He had also taught construction courses at Morton Community College, and he was a consultant with the state construction board. He looked good on paper, and he didn't disappoint anyone on his personal interview. He looked really good. Tappan and the others asked him if he was willing to relocate soon to take a position with a salary that had to be less than he had received in industry. He assured them that he was ready to move next week if they wanted him. He also said that he had read the announcement and it had indicated a salary range. He would expect to be at the top of the range, but he was well aware of the salary possibilities and that he had applied for the job on his own—no one asked him to. Angell detailed his experience, which seemed to be very close to that required in the position of building inspector. He assured the city officials that when his company presented a job to the Morton city inspectors, it was his hide if anything—and he meant anything—did not pass muster.

After the experience with the first ten applicants, the clerk had to ask about the exams. The clerk said, "We have these exams that a building inspector must pass—electrical, plumbing, construction materials. Have you passed the exams?"

John Angell sort of laughed and said, "Well, I thought you read my application before you invited me in, but let me answer you anyway. In a word, the answer is 'Yes.' But maybe you want more than a word. My resumé shows that I teach construction courses at Morton Community College. I teach courses to students who are seeking to pass the electrical, plumbing, and construction materials examinations. In a sense, I teach the examinations." He added, "But more than that, I work for the state construction board. I help the board design the examinations. Also, so you don't get the wrong idea, the exams are graded blindly—we don't know the name of the person taking the exam—but I grade the examinations for the state construction board. Back to the basic question—Yes, I have passed the exams. Moreover, if I do get this job, I would request permission of the city to continue my consulting work with the state board."

Another question was asked about Angell's general health, his ability to climb ladders, and so forth. He answered the questions in a way that gave everyone confidence that he would be able to do the job. He also indicated that he was a by the book enforcer, that builders would have the same book of rules, and they would be expected to conform to each and every rule in the book.

When Angell left, Tappan and his two colleagues gave a collective sigh. This guy was great. This guy was perfect. This guy was just too good. They all thought the same thing, "Was this guy just too good to be true?" All three agreed that he was their first choice, and that they should hire him as soon as possible. Nonetheless, the three agreed that Tappan would call each of his references.

The references just made him seem better than he was at the interview. The director of the state construction board gave him rave reviews. He indicated that the board had made several major changes in policies improving the construction atmosphere in the state precisely because of initiatives taken by Angell. The director insisted that he would like Angell to remain as their consultant and that the city would be honored to have him continuing in that role. The chairman of the construction department at Morton Community College let out an expletive when Tappan informed him that Angell had applied for the Shadford job. "Hey, I'll make you a deal. If I say he stinks, will you pass him by? I don't want to lose him. He is the best instructor we have ever had—that goes back 20 years—in our department—the best!" And so it went. Angell was too good.

Tappan talked to each member of the board, and they all were unanimous that Angell should be offered the job. But they still wanted to wait, they were not sure just for what, but they wanted some more assurances that things were in order. He was too good. Tappan was in a quandary, but he thought he should talk with Bob Slauson, the fire marshal, again. Slauson agreed that Angell was just too good. When Tappan asked if Slauson, who had law enforcement credentials, could use police resources to check him out further, he demurred. He indicated to Tappan that it would be illegal to do so. Besides, on his application, Angell indicated that he had never had any infractions of the law other than minor traffic offenses, and they had checked out his criminal record. He was clean. Slauson did indicate that he worked with fire marshals around the state, and although it wasn't proper, he could make a few private phone calls. Tappan told Slauson that if there was ever any trouble about him doing so, whether it was an ethical violation of technically a legal violation, Slauson was authorized to say that he was ordered by Tappan to make the calls. Tappan even wrote a short memo that Slauson could hold on to saying just that.

Slauson made some calls. The next day he came to Tappan's office with a big smile. "You have your man. He is good, good, good, for the job." Slauson then indicated several problem areas unrelated to the job. Angell had gone through a bitter divorce, and he really wanted to leave town, because both he and his wife had too many mutual friends, and his grown children were getting into the middle of bad situations constantly. Perhaps the divorce had origins in his drinking behavior. Angell was an alcoholic. He didn't drink on the job, but drink-related problems caused him to lose his position with the manufacturing company. He was in the midst of a lawsuit over his firing. He was an alcoholic, but he did not drink. He was a group leader in Alcoholics Anonymous. He counseled others to stop drinking. He had been dry for 7 years. Slauson also found out that Angell had a girlfriend. She lived just a few miles out of Shadford. She, too, had been though a divorce. Her former husband was quite affluent, and she had ample resources to support herself and also Angell if necessary. So Angell's salary was not an issue. What was an issue was the fact that he was driving a 400-mile round trip each week to see his girlfriend.

Tappan was extremely discreet as he shared this information selectively. The girlfriend item was all that some commissioners needed to know, and that was told to them confidentially. The clerk heard the whole story and with a nod he let others know that Angell was O.K. He was hired at the maximum salary authorized in the job announcement.

Angell was not a disappointment. He was energetic. He was a refreshing part of the city hall scene. He soon introduced all the officials and staff to his fiancée. Four months later they were married. While he was not a disappointment, not everyone loved Angell. He went by the book, and he started noting multiple violations for one building project after another. In one case, he made a builder pull out over forty 22-inch-wide windows from an apartment project because the code called for 26-inch-wide windows. Complaints started rolling in to the city mayor's office. Complaints came in to each commissioner. The commission was empowered to review such complaints and change them. But in every case the commission voted six to zero, with one abstention from the builder-commissioner, in favor of Angell. He was simply right in every case.

While the word was getting around, complaints continued to flow in. The commission decided to utilize a state statute that allowed them to appoint a building inspector board of appeals just so they could pass the business on to others. The appeals board sided with Angell every time.

Gradually the complaints subsided. Then a strange thing happened. Several calls came to Tappan's office. They were builders who were praising Angell. The gist of the calls went something like this: "You got a great building inspector with Angell. You know that so-in-so that builds down the street has been cheating for years? I can't compete if you allow him to cheat the way he's been doing. But, boy, I'll tell you, Angell has stopped him cold. We all love him. Keep him; he's a winner."

Six months into the job, Angell was given a 20% merit pay raise, and Tappan told him to pick out a new car—a car was part of the compensation package. He didn't buy an expensive car, but it had a sporty look—a car his new wife would be happy riding in. Angell remained active as a consultant with the state construction board and the city received kudos for allowing him time off for state duties. Angell was active in a state building association, and he invited Tappan to a state meeting. At the meeting Tappan offered to buy Angell a drink. Angell asked for tomato juice; Tappan had a beer.

The city also allowed Angell to teach a course each term at nearby Packard Community College. Tappan also found out indirectly that Angell was involved in leading a local chapter of Alcoholics Anonymous. The next year Tappan found out that Eberbach, the old building inspector, had taken a job as the inspector for a smaller city in the next county. Tappan was relieved that he had not been asked to make a recommendation.

Questions

1. Should the city officials have revealed the truth about the apartment fire and accepted the adverse consequences of a bad insurance rating if they were held liable for the damages?

2. Should Angell have been asked questions about his personal life even though it would have violated personnel policy and even the law?

3. Should the fire marshal have made calls to friends regarding Angell's personal life?

4. Should Angell have been told that Tappan and Slauson had checked out his background?

5. Should the commissioners have been given all the extraneous facts about Angell's background?

6. Should Tappan have offered to buy Angell a drink at the state conference knowing what he knew about Angell's alcoholism?

Chapter 13

Loose Lips Sink Ships and Can Hurt in Other Ways, Too

"A long habit of not thinking a thing wrong gives it a superficial appearance of being right."

—**Tom Paine**

Professional positions demand the utmost in discretion. Even an innocent remark made to another professional employee at the wrong time can have dire consequences. Such was the case when Sergeant Dave Ulrich of the Baldwin Village police force overheard a remark at the Montclair Tavern. The Montclair was the natural gathering place for off-duty members of the Baldwin force, thirty strong, as it was only three blocks from the village hall, but it was located outside the village in the city of Granger.

Ulrich had grown up in Baldwin, on the same block as Police Chief Hugh Overbeck. They went to elementary school, middle school, and high school together. Each was very active in school sports and by high school they had become rivals. Indeed they were very antagonistic towards one another. The antagonism only grew as both were rookies on the Baldwin force together. Overbeck was the consummate politician, while Ulrich never held back his feelings, and called a spade a spade, as it were. After 15 years on the force, Ulrich had enjoyed one promotion to the rank of sergeant, while Overbeck had successfully used his cool manner to win support not only for three promotions, but for the achievement of the post of village chief of police.

Overbeck was not exactly a good winner in his lifelong competition with Ulrich. As chief, he seem to enjoy riding him, with demerits for miniscule infractions such as having a shirt button unbuttoned or having his hair a bit longer than regulations required.

George Slater was elected village president in the fall elections, upsetting a two-term incumbent. He did not learn about the animosity between Ulrich and Overbeck until he had been in office almost 3 months.

There was a hostage crisis at Borders Hospital, and Ulrich led the contingent of village officers at the site. Ulrich personally talked a gunman into a peaceful surrender just outside of the maternity ward. The news media had footage of Ulrich slowly and carefully walking up to the gun-carrying man and talking him into handing over the weapon, after which other officers put handcuffs on the man.

It sure appeared that Ulrich had engaged in above-and-beyond duty, and President Slater wanted the village council to recognize him for his brave act. Slater wrote a resolution of praise and it was printed on an appropriate scroll. When the item of recognition appeared on the village board agenda, Chief Overbeck made a visit to Slater's office. Overbeck, in his gentle and suave way, began to describe what had appeared on the news screens of the village and nearby city of Granger as something quite different. He indicated that Ulrich was part of a larger team that went to the hospital, and that it was another officer who had negotiated with the gunman, and that Ulrich was only the one who took the gun away. Slater thanked the chief for the explanation. However, Slater kept the resolution on the agenda, and the village board and the audience at the meeting gave Ulrich a rousing round of applause as he received his scroll with the commendation. Slater asked the other village officers about the chief's conversation with him, and he was given more details of the rivalry between Ulrich and Overbeck. Slater hoped that the two would outgrow the rivalry or at least that it would be manifested in rather minor skirmishes such as awards and demerits. His hopes were dashed as the hot, humid summer descended over the Midwestern village.

Gail Wahr was the county district attorney. He had just been elected by the largest margin in history. All eyes were on Wahr, as people had him pegged to be a future congressman or maybe attorney general or governor. He was a rising star. Wahr was an activist and a go-getter. He was a no-nonsense crime buster. Wahr also socialized with county law enforcement staff. At a social occasion, he was tipping drinks with Susan Gill. Susan worked for the child welfare division, and discussion turned to child molesters.

"Talk about headaches," Wahr exclaimed, "We have a doozy." He then said he couldn't talk about it, but it was close to home, and some county people were going to feel it when it came out. The drinks kept coming, and Gill was anxious to find out more about what the district attorney had said. He kept brushing her off, but then casually said the matter involved a police officer in the county sexually assaulting his 13-year-old daughter.

Gill had a boyfriend, Tom Van Buren, who just happened to be the bartender at the Montclair Tavern. Susan came in regularly. She happened to come in right after the county social gathering. While she waited for Van Buren to get off work, she had a few drinks. In the course of the drinking session, she said, "D.A. Wahr is investigating charges that a local policeman is molesting his 13-year-old daughter."

These were loose words, not loudly said, but nonetheless they reached the nearby ears of Ulrich. He heard them clearly, one time. That was enough. It was like a sledgehammer that had been raised over his head for 3 decades came down crushing against his skull, leaving him seriously wounded but still on his feet and still able to strike back. Strike back he did, first verbally, then with threats, and finally with a rush out the door, proclaiming that he was going to the village hall to kill the chief. It happened that Ulrich had a 13-year-old daughter.

Before he left, he was screaming, "That bastard, first he tries to demote me . . . he's tried to fire me ten times, but now he's going after my family, my God! Accusing me of molesting my daughter. How low can a person go? I'll kill that bastard!" Then he grabbed the telephone and called the village police office and repeated his ranting, all of which were peppered with the most gross of profanities. Tom yelled at him to put the phone down. "You're not calling the police line are you?"

"Damn right I am."

"But Dave, it's all recorded," Van Buren replied.

Ulrich answered, "I don't give a f——," and he continued his diatribe. As Ulrich left the Tavern, Van Buren quickly phoned the police station to warn officers that Ulrich was coming, and to make sure the chief got out of there safely and quickly.

Fortunately, the chief had left for the day, so Ulrich's antics at the police station just consisted of more verbal tirades, filled with venom and more profanities. After Sergeant Ulrich left, the chief was contacted, and a patrol car was sent to make sure he was safe. The police also kept general track of Ulrich. Luckily, he decided to go home.

The next day, the word spread rather quickly around the village hall. The chief called Village President Slater and asked that he gather the village clerk and treasurer for a quick meeting. He added that it was a personnel matter, so they didn't have to worry about the state open meetings law. The chief and a deputy brought the village officers the telephone recordings. They were devastating.

All at the meeting were stunned. What should they do next? A very delicate call to a person in the know at the district attorney's office confirmed that an investigation of the type referred to was indeed taking place. However, the object of the investigation was a county deputy who was assigned to the corrections division—the county jail. The D.A.'s remarks had nothing to do with Sergeant Ulrich or Chief Overbeck.

Nonetheless, the rivalry of Ulrich and Overbeck had to come to an end. President Slater said what all knew—it was a very unfortunate situation, but Ulrich's police career was probably at an end. However, Slater did not want to rush to a decision. He felt that Ulrich deserved that they not judge him hastily. Slater proposed that Ulrich be put on immediate 2-week leave, with full pay. That would give them all time to consider the right steps to take. Friends of Ulrich within the police force were able to get the truth to him, so that he knew that the chief had never accused Ulrich of any seriously improper of illegal behavior. Ulrich wasn't going to apologize, but he let his friends know that he had lost it, and he wasn't mad at the chief, and that he had acted inappropriately. The chief had a member of the force who was a good friend of Ulrich visit his home and request his gun. This was done peacefully.

The next week, a sporting goods store that sold merchandise to most amateur teams in the village of Baldwin and in the city of Granger made a offer to hire Ulrich as a salesman. Ulrich had been very active in amateur and youth sports. The store owner was a friend of his. He took the job and informed the village that he intended to retire. Ulrich was able to retire with a clean record. The village officials made a solid mental note of what had happened, but as far as any record went, the books were closed. Ulrich was in no mood to seek another law enforcement position, and he did not do so. Ulrich did not have any kind of formal retirement party, but his friends did gather around him at the Montclair Tavern to offer support. When the village recreation program needed supplies the next summer, the director made sure he placed an order with Ulrich.

Questions

1. Could this story have had any other ending?
2. When a law enforcement official shares inside information, even with another professional employee, should the official be specific so that the information will not be misused?
3. Should law enforcement officials socialize with one another?
4. Did the village have an obligation to intervene in the Ulrich–Overbeck animosity situation much earlier?
5. To what extent did the village or the county have an obligation to assure that Ulrich had some kind of job after his blowup?
6. Should criminal action have been taken against Ulrich?
7. Should disciplinary action have been taken against the district attorney or against the child welfare officer, Gill?

Chapter 14

Peter, Paul, and Mary: Ethical Quandaries or Managerial Issues?

"Gratitude is not only the greatest of virtues, but the parent of all the others."

—**Cicero**

The Peter, Paul, and Mary Principles

In 1969, Laurence J. Peter and Raymond Hull penned their classic, *The Peter Principle*.[1] They cautioned readers that they would immediately be pointing fingers at others, but before they did so, they should look into the mirror. Incompetence is not a quality that only some possess. We all may possess the quality at some time. First the authors defined their terms. The competent person is the one who gets the job done (effectiveness) with the resources at hand (efficiency)—this they called producing the output. The competent person does the work while abiding by organizational rules and procedures—this they called the input of the job. Over time

---

[1]Peter, Laurence J. and Raymond Hull. *The Peter Principle*. New York: W. Morrow, 1969.

some people come to be promoted into new jobs with new demands, and some of these people cease to produce output. Either they do not get the job done at all, or they cannot do it with the resources available. They have become incompetent. However, they still abide by the input requirements of the job—they obey the rules and they follow proper procedures. In other words, they can't do the work, but they show up on time. Because most workers are judged on input factors, the incompetent person will not lose the new position, but he or she will stay there forever; their lack of output will preclude further promotions.

There are corollaries of the Peter Principle. Peter and Hull speculate that we all get promoted, and we all finally come to a level on the hierarchy where we are incompetent, and we just stay there, and so in time every position in every organization becomes filled with an incompetent person. Hence, all of society is going to hell in a handbag.

There are other takes on the concept of incompetence. Paul Armour formulated the *Paul Principle*.[2] He reasoned that a competent person could, over time, become incompetent without having been promoted. Time changes the qualities necessary to do a job; time also introduces changes in personality including resentments over not being promoted, burnout caused by competing obligations (growing families, etc.), and the tiring factors of aging. Again, we are left with the corollaries that lead to the conclusion that all organizations are filling up with incompetent people.

Who is left to do the work? How about a person who is not promoted, but at the same time is pampered with good social and physical working conditions, pay raises, praise, and most of all, retraining? Maybe someone named *Mary*, The Management Assistant—the person we used to call "secretary."

In his term of office as mayor of the city of Brighton, Kent Chartwell interacted with people at various stages of the Peter, Paul, and Mary charts of competence. He had a chance to wonder if the principles involving work efforts and competence were ethical factors or simply management issues. Perhaps the reader could advise him on an answer to that question.

Case 1–Peter

Dover Fife was a lieutenant on the Brighton police force. He had joined the force 35 years previously when it had only four members. From the beginning, it seemed that he always had more seniority than anyone else, and the longevity must have proven useful in his career development. In 15 years he rose to the rank of sergeant, then to the rank of lieutenant, and then he found himself the third-highest-ranking offi-

[2]Loven, John. The MPA Team Spirit Newsletter, June 2004. See www.mrateamspirit.com/pages/news letter01.asp.

cer among the 35 on the force. He had just turned 60, but the city had 5 years earlier eliminated its mandatory retirement age, so he had no plans for moving on. Only one other member of the force was as old as Fife. No one on the force could remember when Fife was an effective or competent employee. He may or may not have had abilities when he was younger. The Peter Principle may have eaten him up, but no one wanted to try him out as a patrolman to see. It is more likely that he was "Pauled out" early in the game. He had become fat and slow with age; he had lost all sense of being assertive. Maybe he was also resentful that a much younger man, Ansell Henry, had passed him by to become chief. Fife would be the only one to think any injustice had been done there. He put in his time, but Chartwell wondered, and Chief Henry wondered, if Fife's time on the job was a complete waste of time, indeed a waste of a life. They felt Fife would be more productive if he were fishing or watching cartoons on television.

What was the force to do about Fife? The authors of the Peter Principle suggest one strategy for dealing with the incompetent. They call it the lateral arabesque. In this strategy, the organization seeks to find some work where the person can be occupied and do very little harm in the process. Hence Fife was made the special ordinance enforcement officer. His duties included giving tickets or warnings (he was afraid to confront most citizens with tickets); for burning trash in the open; for having visible trash in their yards; for having nonoperating automobiles in their driveways, on the street, or on their grass; and assisting the animal control department if it called and another officer was not available. It was not a hard job, but someone had to do it—maybe not a high ranking full-time someone, but someone.

Chief Henry also sent Fife to various meetings where it was requested that the city be represented, but the meeting did not seem to be important or worth the time of a real officer. Fife attended a meeting sponsored by the state director of emergency planning one day, and he came back with some intriguing news. The city did not have a city civil defense director. Not only that, but if the city appointed one, the federal government would provide one half of the salary for the position. Henry asked what the duties of the post were, and Fife pulled out a pamphlet that said the civil defense director would be a critical officer if there ever were an enemy attack, and that the director would be in charge of getting housing for people in wartime emergencies and other disasters. Henry called Mayor Chartwell's office and told the mayor to come on down for a quick chat. Henry dismissed Fife and then told the mayor that they might just have a solution for Fife. He could work on civil defense planning, be out of their hair, and the federal government would foot half the bill. All they had to do was create a post of civil defense director. Chartwell agreed to call the city attorney to make sure no other township duties would be shifted if they gave the post to Fife. They were all happy that the position seemed to require attendance at a lot of meetings. The city council seemed to go along with the solution to a Peter and Paul problem. A few grumbled that they should just fire the old man, but they restrained themselves from saying it too loud. A perfect lateral arabesque. The job was created, and the appointment was made.

For the next 2 or 3 months, Fife was seen every few days with papers and maps in his hands. Chartwell asked him how things were going, and he was so happy to tell him about the job. "You know, we are O.K. if the Russians put a bomb on St. Louis, 'cause all the people there are going to head over toward Harding, but if the bomb goes in Chicago, they will be coming this direction and on to Wilson. But we have to be able to take care of an additional 15,000 people—why, that's nearly half again our population. I got to find places for all these people." The next week he announced that he was going to every church within 10 miles to see about basement space. And so it appeared that Peter's final placement for Lieutenant Fife was turning out well.

Well? Not quite. But Chartwell and Henry gave it little thought. They were two busy beavers on June 13, when a major tornado ripped into one side of the city and out the other, leaving signs of destruction over a 5-mile pathway. Sixty houses were destroyed. Three churches were leveled; the business district looked like a war zone. Broken trees blocked all the major streets. The full police department was deployed and all fire personnel called to duty. Door-to-door searches were made of all houses. Unfortunately, four persons were found dead. It was a long night, and Fife came by the station, so Chartwell had Fife drive him through the hardest hit areas. He forgot Fife after that. Indeed, he didn't see him for 4 days.

The clean-up crews were organized by the mayor in cooperation with Chief Henry, and a plan of cleaning up the streets took shape. The mayor engaged federal officials about declarations of emergency and then setting up offices where residents could begin a process of seeking loans for rebuilding. The mayor also coordinated the organization of a central office for insurance agents. A special city council meeting was called regarding an application for federal aid to offset municipal government costs.

An announcement on the radio told the citizens that the National Guard was coming into the area. The citizens started calling to ask when the National Guard was going to clean up their streets and when the National Guard was going to open buildings. The mayor called a radio station and the announcer just said he read the report on the wire. The mayor asked Chief Henry. He said he sure would like to know; his police were fully deployed, and officers were getting by on 4 hours of sleep, as he had them working 20-hour shifts. He also had them guarding areas against looting, and they had specific orders to keep all unidentified people out of residential neighborhoods. Henry was concerned that the National Guard might just show up and screw all their plans up. He was exasperated. "It's a hell of a way to run a National Guard. Why don't you call them?" he asked Chartwell.

Chartwell was unsure who to call at the state capital, so when he got through to the National Guard, he just said, "I'm the mayor of Brighton, and I want the adjutant general." His call was placed right through to the top military man in the state. Chartwell was impressed, but he was also disturbed, so he vented on the general, "We keep hearing you are coming, but we have a job to do. Now if you are coming, it would be nice if my police chief and I could be clued in on things, don't you think?"

The general was probably a bit older than Mayor Chartwell, because his voice had a bit of condescension in it as he replied. "Young man, you have had a disaster, and we are here to help you. But I do not understand your call and your tone. We have been in constant contact with your office from 1 hour after that tornado ripped through your city."

Chartwell was dumbfounded, but he thought he had better let the general speak on.

The general continued, "I have personally had six conversations with your civil defense director, Lieutenant Fife. I have given him up-to-date information about all our activities and when we expect to be in your area, and our troop strength. I would advise you to talk to your own people before you call me."

Chartwell could only say, "I am very sorry about my tone, sir. Thank you for all you are doing. I understand your situation. Please, my apologies and thank you. Good-bye."

Chief Henry and Mayor Chartwell stayed 24 hours a day at the city hall, grabbing a few hours of sleep on a cot, in frequent contact with police and fire officers. Yet to the state military department, Lieutenant Fife, the civil defense director, was in charge of all city activities regarding the tornado.

Fife showed up 4 days later. He indicated that after he had driven around the city with the mayor, his stomach began to ache, so he went home. During the ride he had neglected to tell the mayor that he had had a call from the adjutant general of the state, asking what kind of troop strength would be available to help for backup. After he went home, he received five other calls from the state capital, but he had not thought it necessary to relay the details of those calls to either the mayor or the police chief, because, "after all, the calls were for me; I am the civil defense director."

A month later, Mayor Chartwell asked the city treasurer to draw up a retirement portfolio for all city employees over 60 years old. It would tell them what they would expect in retirement pay and Social Security if they left their jobs then. He asked the treasurer to make an addendum indicating what they would receive at age 63 and age 65. The treasurer was to leave that addendum off the report given to Lieutenant Fife. Instead, Fife's report was to have a statement regarding the pay he would be receiving if he continued working versus the pay he would receive in retirement, and a statement to show the difference. It turned out that Fife was effectively working for a mere 24¢ more each hour on the job than he would receive in retirement. There was also a statement for Fife regarding a healthcare supplement he would receive until he took Medicare. After the statements were mailed, Chief Henry asked Fife if he got his retirement planning memo. He then added that Fife's job duties would probably be changing—that he might be out on patrol duty more as they need several more officers on traffic duty. Also, the chief said one of the night shift officers was leaving the force, and he might have to ask everyone to fill in for a few months at a time with night duty. Fife decided to take retirement.

Case 2–Paul

Mayor Chartwell's third month in office brought a pleasant surprise. Marion Meriwether appeared at his door, as if out of the blue. She was an education major at the local university specializing in recreation programs for children. She was the personification of enthusiasm. She asked Chartwell if they had a summer parks recreation program for the city. The mayor replied that they had a program of some sort and that they had a director, Winston Battle, a local schoolteacher. However, the mayor had not yet met Battle personally. The mayor suggested that there was always room for new ideas, and since he had not heard much about the program, perhaps it wasn't too developed. He asked Meriwether if she had any ideas. The question was like turning on the fountain—or the waterfalls. Meriwether just started rolling out ideas seemingly off the top of her head. The kids could go to the zoo in the next city. They could go to the cookie factory, maybe to a baseball game in St. Louis or Chicago. Meriwether continued, discussing new crafts ideas, painting, game tournaments, clown days, and amateur music festivals. Chartwell was bowled over, to use a recreational term.

Chartwell talked with Meriwether some more, and then invited her to lunch along with some other officials. Later he asked that she send him her college transcript, so that he could see all the courses she had taken, and he asked if she would consider being a codirector or assistant director to Battle. She nearly jumped out of her seat when he mentioned this. Chartwell told her that he would set up an appointment for both of them to meet with Battle for some afternoon soon.

It was Chartwell's first meeting with Battle. He introduced himself and then he introduced Meriwether. He asked Battle to describe some of the duties he had as a recreational director and to tell them about the program. In doing so, Battle made the program seem very passive, and, to Chartwell, boring. Battle indicated that about ten kids came daily to each of four locations around the city. Battle recruited eight students to work as recreational assistants during summer months. The mayor then asked Meriwether to share some of her ideas with Battle. She whirled off about ten new ideas hardly containing her enthusiasm. When she was done, Chartwell asked Battle if he thought that her ideas could be fit into the program and if he would be interested in having Meriwether as his assistant or even codirector, understanding that his pay for the summer job would remain the same. Battle was told that it was his program, so really it was his call.

Battle looked at the mayor, and he said, "Oh, I think I'll take a pass."

The mayor was not exactly sure what that meant. He asked Battle if that meant he didn't want to make any changes, or he didn't want Meriwether's help.

Battle replied, "No, I just mean that maybe there's too much work in the program. You know, good luck, but hey that's a lot on the plate. I really have doubts we can do all those things. Maybe I'll just pass on running the program this year. I won't have to worry about when I take off for our family vacation this way. I think you have the person you want anyway."

Chartwell insisted that he wanted to keep Battle, but he sensed that all along he had been implying that the position of summer recreational director would entail some work in the coming summer. Battle was not up to the idea of work. After all he was a teacher, and they were talking about his summer vacation. The mayor had seen Meriwether's transcript, and he had called a few of her professors. He was convinced that he had discovered a jewel. As soon as Battle left, he offered her the position.

It was now quite apparent to Chartwell that Battle had been holding the summer job for several years just to pad his personal payroll. While in some cases humanitarian motivations may cause leaders to retain nonproductive personnel who had performed well in the past, this was not such a case. Battle had another job, and Chartwell had constituents who deserved to have effective programs. Meriwether was a person who could deliver for the city's children.

Over the next three summers, the city recreation program flourished, winning accolades from citizens and recreational professionals throughout the area. Meriwether went door to door with pamphlets about the program. She expanded it to six playgrounds at parks and schools. Each playground area was filled with three dozen or so kids every day. Local merchants made donations of prizes for games, and Meriwether started a donation fund so the kids got free refreshments. A highlight of the first summer was John Little Day, held during the All-Star break, at a play area that was next to Central High School. Little had achieved local fame when he led the Central Pioneers to their only state title in baseball, and he had since then become a major league ballplayer. He came, signed autographs, gave away two dozen baseballs in a raffle, and gave a motivational speech. Over ninety kids came to the event, which was covered in all the local news media. It was a roaring success.

Chartwell realized that if he had a job that demanded a lot of work to be done well, he should give the job to a busy person, not to Paul.

Case 3—Mary

Anne Canterbury was not a victim of the Peter Principle or the Paul Principle. Instead she more closely personified the Mary Principle. Canterbury and the clerical staff of the city kept the local government engine running. They held its organizational memory. They knew where all the forms were hidden, and they knew who to call each time an official had to put out a proverbial brush fire. If treated right, if given retraining on all the new machines and all the new skills and techniques of clerical life, if compensated fairly, and if allowed ample time for socializing before and after work and on breaks, the Marys of the world would continue to be the ones getting the work done when all those about them had succumbed to the affliction of incompetence.

However, there is a fear in organizations regarding training and retraining. Very few local governments and even business organizations see the value of investing training money in their staffs. After hiring is over, almost 100% of training is on-the-job training. Training is the key to heading off the disasters that occur with the onset of Paul and Peter Principle syndromes. Yet most organizations are afraid to make the investment. Managers at most organizations think that training only produces situations like that experienced with Sam Bruckerhoff, a friend of mayor Chartwell, who, like Canterbury personified the Mary Principle.

After several failed attempts to achieve a college degree and several tries in management trainee positions to no avail, Bruckerhoff was persuaded by an agent at Stanley, Fenner, and Lynch to take an exam to see if he could become a stockbroker. He passed the exam. Stanley, Fenner, and Lynch then put him on its payroll and sent him off to New York City for 6 weeks of training. Bruckerhoff actually received part of his training on the floor of the New York Stock Exchange. He came back to Brighton with an excitement he had never felt before. He was then given his new "work manual"—the phone book. He was told to make cold calls to all the names from G to N. Bruckerhoff even got Chartwell to come to his office and purchase a few stocks. But when Chartwell called to do lunch a month later, Bruckerhoff was not there. The person on the other end of the line said the Bruckerhoff was no longer with Stanley, Fenner, and Lynch. He couldn't say where Bruckerhoff was. Chartwell called Bruckerhoff at home later the same evening. Bruckerhoff told him that the local stock firm of Norman and Williams had called him and asked if he would like to join their staff.

Bruckerhoff said his initial reply had been, "Yeah, and what are you promising me, the *R*s, *S*s, and *T*s?"

This was not the case. A Norman and Williams salesman had retired and moved to Florida. Sam could take over and service 220 of his 240 clients. These 220 were already stock owners. He would be servicing them (as in "churning"); he would not have to sell them any stocks. Sam left Stanley, Fenner, and Lynch the next day, and all their training investment went to a competitor.

The city of Brighton did not think of training costs as a negative factor. Mayor Chartwell knew they had better train someone to operate the new computers that would track all city records and tax payments. Chartwell thought that Canterbury was the person to do the job. She was loyal and she was energetic. She was a single mother who had struggled to take care of her kids and to better herself professionally. Everyone liked her.

Canterbury was deserving of any chance she could get to advance her professional talents. Chartwell asked her if she would like to go to a training program in North Carolina for two weeks. She showed interest. Chartwell told her that the city would pay the cost of the computer course, transportation, and the cost of an upgraded room at the Ramada Inn on the ocean in Wilmington. She could charge all her meals as well. She would be on salary for the 2 weeks plus 2 days, and the city would also give her $300 extra if she wanted to stay in the beach community for a few extra days. She would be expected to attend all of the 10 days of sessions of the computer course. She liked the arrangements, and Chartwell enrolled her in the course.

Canterbury was very happy when she returned from North Carolina. She was chatting with everyone in the office about her trip. Everyone was laughing with her as she described a guy she met. Canterbury greeted Chartwell when he came in the city hall office area at 8:30 AM on her first day back in the office, and she said she wanted to have a meeting with him. At 9:30 AM she went into his office. Chartwell asked her about the training, and her responses confirmed that she had worked hard during the course and she was indeed ready to be the person in charge of data input and retrieval from the new computers that were to be delivered soon.

She then bluntly said, "I want a raise."

"Wow," was the mayor's response. "All staff received raises 3 months ago, and will quite likely get cost-of-living raises next year. What do you want now, and why?"

"Well," she responded, "I am now a computer technician."

The mayor said that when the computers were finally installed, they could reevaluate her job grade for the following year, or perhaps a bit sooner.

"Yes," she said, "that is all well and good, but today I can get a job paying me 20% more than I'm getting now. I can be a computer operator. The job was offered to me after the training course."

Chartwell asked where the job was, and Canterbury replied that it was in North Carolina. By the time of that discussion, Chartwell had heard about the guy in North Carolina. Chartwell told her that it is nice to be wanted, and asked if she wanted to move to North Carolina. Canterbury replied that things could really be neat in other places.

Chartwell replied, "Hey, if you really want to pursue a dream, I guess all I can say is Godspeed, good luck. Do you *really* want to move to North Carolina?" Canterbury answered that she did not, but boy it sounded good. Chartwell told her that if she stayed and did her job well, good things would happen in time, maybe even in a short time. But there was to be no raise at this time. Over the next week Canterbury shared that the guy who offered her the job was really neat, but married.

Canterbury stayed in Brighton, and the next year her job was reclassified and she received a base raise of 10% above what she had been receiving. The Mary Principle survived.

Questions

1. Why is there an organizational reluctance to fire incompetent employees, especially those who have given long service?

2. Was it unethical for the city of Brighton to take money from the federal government to pay an incompetent employee?

3. Were Brighton officials being incompetent in the way they resolved the situation with Dover Fife?

4. Shouldn't the city officials had known that Fife was being given powers in all disaster situations, not just at times of nuclear attack?

5. Is it unethical to assign make-work tasks to an incompetent worker instead of relieving him of his job?

6. How could the state National Guard have been assured that its calls were reaching the proper authorities in the city of Brighton? Was that its duty?

7. Is it unethical to let a service program, like the recreational program, linger just because the person in charge lacks energy to make it work?

8. Should Chartwell merely have replaced Battle with Meriwether, instead of giving him the choice to remain in charge?

9. Bruckerhoff's actions toward Stanley, Fenner, and Lynch appear to be disloyal to say the least, but were they unethical?

10. Were Stanley, Fenner, and Lynch disloyal to Bruckerhoff by just throwing him a phone book and telling him that was his work manual?

11. How could Stanley, Fenner, and Lynch have been assured that their training budget wasn't a total waste?

12. The city of Brighton paid for Canterbury's training; is it ethical of her to demand a pay raise because of the training?

13. Would it be ethical for the city of Brighton to pay Canterbury more because she had been offered a job elsewhere? Would this be an invitation for all other staff members to seek other jobs?

14. What might officials in Brighton think about training courses for their employees in the future?

Chapter 15

Elected Officials at Work and/or Play

"You cannot make yourself feel something you do not feel, but you can make yourself do right in spite of your feelings."

—Pearl Buck

The introduction to this book begs the question, "Are there different ethical standards for elected officials than appointed ones?" In their text; *Public Administration, Power and Politics in the Fourth Branch of Government*, Smith and Licari offer a traditional definition of ethics as "A system of behavior based on values and moral principles designed to help people distinguish between right and wrong behavior."[1] In the case study presented here, we will examine the ethics of elected officials with an emphasis on their moral principles and their own morality. While we will find that they are held to a different ethical standard, we will discover that the standard is not necessarily higher or even equal.

Brent Township is located adjacent to a large urban center in a major metropolitan region. Matt Beckman had served 13 years as the township manager. During his

[1]Smith, Kevin B. and Licari, Michael J. *Public Administration, Power and Politics in the Fourth Branch of Government*. Los Angeles: Roxbury, 2006, p. 119.

tenure, he saw a cast of characters come into and out of elected positions with the township. Some were professional—lawyers, architects, engineers, and the like, while others were more the blue collar, working class type. Some of their antics were humorous and some exposed the township to considerable liability. One of the more astute trustees arrived at the township hall one day at Christmastime dressed in his full regalia as Santa Claus. He demanded permission to go from office to office to solicit donations for the local Goodfellows so that every child could have a Christmas. When Manager Beckman told him that that was against township policy, he demanded to know, "Says who?" Even though this Santa was one of his bosses, Beckman stuck to his guns. Santa stumped and harrumphed out of the offices mumbling, "We'll see about this," with his bells jingling all the way.

Another trustee was noted for his command of the English language . . . he could barely speak in complete sentences. At one particular board meeting he prefaced his remarks on some profound pronouncement he was about to offer by saying, "Don't quote me. I am going to speak verbatim now."

One newly elected township clerk, who was responsible for all accounts payable, nearly cost the township $250,000 in fines and penalties for failing to remit employee income tax withholdings to the state for the 6 months she had been in office. When confronted by Beckman, she opened a drawer in her desk filled with forms sent to her by the state. She was supposed to complete them and send them back to the state with a check for the withholding amount. Asked why she had not done this, her response was that she did not know how to fill those complicated forms out. Her experience in finance prior to being elected was that of a homemaker and even she agreed she could not balance the family checkbook. In her own defense, she said that sooner or later she was going to ask someone how to fill them out. "I was going to get around to it," she insisted.

Due to some swift action by Beckman and after pleading relentlessly with the state, the state waived the fines and penalty. Beckman had successfully argued that the taxpayers of Brent Township should not be penalized for the ineptness and incompetence of one of their elected officials (even though they elected her).

These, and many others, prove that anyone can be elected to public office. The only qualifications are that a candidate be 18 years of age, reside in the community for the office he or she is seeking, and be alive. There are no other prerequisites. In the state where Brent Township is located, even convicted felons, unless they are incarcerated, are eligible for elective office, including those of the governor and elected county sheriff. That is exactly what happened in Washington County, where Brent Township is located. The local sheriff was caught red handed pilfering sides of beef from the county jail, filling up family and friends' cars with county gasoline, and other nefarious deeds. Although his actions constituted felonies, in a plea bargain, he pleaded guilty to a single misdemeanor charge on the condition that he resigned from the sheriff's office. He did not have to serve time in his own jail. He resigned and returned to his prior occupation as a dairy farmer.

Six years later he again ran for county sheriff and handily won. The incumbent sheriff who had been appointed to fill the crooked sheriff's vacancy was an honest fellow but totally incompetent. Two years into his four-year term, the crooked re-elected sheriff did it again. He stole county property, gave gasoline away to family and friends, and even lined his pockets with county money. He once again was forced to resign.

As noted, Brent Township had more than its fair share of colorful characters serve on the township board over the years. Here we examine three trustees in particular: Trustees Bill Curtis, Walt Fenton, and Carl Morgan.

Trustee Curtis

Bill Curtis was an eleventh-grade dropout. He was a self-taught plumber by trade and barely eked out a living as a self-employed businessman. He was serving the first year of his second term on the Brent Township board of trustees when his troubles began.

On a warm summer Monday morning, Brent's police chief informed the township manager that there was a rumor spreading throughout the Department that Trustee Curtis had been arrested the previous Friday afternoon for soliciting a prostitute in the adjoining central urban city. It appeared that the undercover police decoy who caught Mr. Curtis was dating one of Brent's younger officers. Having never been confronted with a situation such as this before, Manager Beckman was uncertain as to how to handle it. He decided to first simply confront Trustee Curtis with the allegation. He called Curtis and advised him of the rumors. Curtis responded, "Rumors, rumors. People spread these all the time. They are just rumors." Beckman advised him that if it was not true, he would let the police department know and put this matter to rest. Again, Curtis responded, "Rumors, just rumors. That's all they are. Just rumors." Curtis did not deny the arrest because he could not. The report of his arrest was true.

Beckman did not feel that it was his job to "keep the puppies in the box," so to speak. He felt that was the job of the board's highest elected official, the township supervisor (the equivalent of a mayor). Supervisor Mark Bailey took Beckman's call in his community college office, where he served as the business administrator. He was somewhat amused over Curtis's predicament. Bailey always thought Curtis was somewhat of a lowlife and his arrest for solicitation just further confirmed it.

Bailey called Curtis and suggested that he meet with him and Manager Beckman at 5:00 PM in his community college office. Curtis refused until Bailey threatened to call an emergency board meeting to address the situation publicly. Curtis arrived at the scheduled time and told the supervisor and manager the following story.

"I was driving down Concord Street [an area known to be frequented by prostitutes] last Friday at about two in the afternoon and I saw this pretty girl standing on a corner . . . *and she was a pretty girl. Very pretty.* I pulled up along side of her and said 'hello,' and she said 'hello' back. I asked her if she wanted a ride and she didn't really answer me. I then offered her $25 and the next thing I know I was in cuffs and in the back seat of a police car. I protested and told them that they couldn't be doing this because I was on the Brent Township board and that I was conducting official township business.

"You guys got to understand I was just checking prices. I just wanted to know how much they charge. You know that these hookers are getting closer and closer to our township borders. I was not planning on doing anything. Just checking prices. Checking prices.

"I sat in the back of the police car for 20 minutes or so, then asked the uniformed officer in the driver's seat what they were doing. He said that they were waiting to catch a couple more of us. After about 10 minutes I leaned forward and said, 'Slow day, isn't it?' And, do you know what he said to me? He told me to shut up. That was rude.

"After they caught a couple of other guys, then they took the three of us to the precinct, which wasn't too far away. When they brought me in, I recognized the desk sergeant. He was one of my neighbors. He told them to let me go and they did."

When pressed and asked if had requested a specific sex act, as the police department had told them, he said, "Yeah, I might have said something like that."

The following day, Manager Beckman and the entire township board were to meet in the state capital for the annual legislative conference sponsored by the State Township Association. Driving alone in his car, Beckman was about halfway to the capital when his pager and cell phone went off at the same time. He was impressed with his importance but disappointed that no one was around to see it. He was being inundated by the metro area's media outlets, both print and broadcast. They had gotten wind of Trustee Curtis's arrest and wanted Beckman's comments. Beckman told all of them he had no comment and they all demanded to speak with the wayward trustee. He told them that he would so advise Mr. Curtis, and he did so when he caught up with him in the capital.

Curtis refused to call the media, saying it was none of their business. He consulted with a trustee from another township as to how he should handle the mess that he had gotten himself into. That trustee advised him to avoid the press at all cost. When he asked if that trustee was an attorney, the trustee replied that, he was a barber.

The media continued to hammer Manager Beckman, accusing him of a coverup. He and Supervisor Bailey finally convinced Curtis to issue a prepared statement and to read it by telephone to a trusted print reporter. They even helped him write the rather bland statement conceding that he had been arrested for accosting and soliciting a prostitute, but arguing that it was all a big misunderstanding. He was told to read the statement to the reporter and then hang up. With his wife at his side (she bought his story about being on official township business), he phoned the reporter.

After reading the prepared statement, he did not do as he was advised. He answered, "Yes," then laughed and said, "31 years." He then cupped his hand over the telephone's mouthpiece, turned to his wife and chuckled, "He wants to know how many years we've been married, honey." Turning back to the phone, he said "Two." Still chuckling, he turned back to his wife and said, "He wants to know how many kids we have." The banter continued back and forth for another 10 minutes as if he were talking to a good friend about a football game.

The township board and a majority of the community was quite upset and disturbed with the embarrassment and disgrace Trustee Curtis had brought upon the township. Demands for his resignation were swift and vocal. Upon returning from the state capital, Curtis did finally consult with an attorney. At the next meeting of the township board, Curtis did not make an appearance. Rather, his attorney delivered his signed resignation from the township board and Curtis faded into the sunset.

He is affectionately remembered as the Solicitor General and his creative economic indicator was dubbed the WPI, or Whore Price Index. Township officials never did quite figure out if it was good, bad, or indifferent if the price of prostitutes was increasing or decreasing as they plied their trade closer to the township's borders.

A year later Curtis was caught soliciting again and was arrested. He did not have a desk sergeant neighbor that time to give him a pass. He was found guilty of the misdemeanor charge and paid a $1,000 fine.

Trustee Fenton

Walt Fenton was making his first venture into the political arena in Brent Township. He campaigned aggressively for a seat on the township board. His professionally prepared campaign flyer touted his qualifications and experience: bachelor's degree in accounting, professional tax advisor, member of the planning commission, active in scouting, board member of an area Catholic high school, and so on. He also noted that he was married and the father of two young boys. Fenton distributed his campaign literature door-to-door for weeks prior to the election. He visited nearly every home in the township at least once and many two or three times. He was well received by most voters and appeared to be an up and coming leader in the community. Over 300 residents allowed him to place Elect Fenton yard signs on their front lawns.

His hard work paid off as he easily won a seat on the township board in his first bid for public office. In an effort to immediately demonstrate his commitment to the community, he decided that he would remove all of his lawn signs the night of the election so that the township would not be littered with them the next day. Prior candidates had taken days or sometime weeks to remove their meaningless signs following an election. It was around midnight when he parked at the entrance of a subdivision and walked to about 20 homes to retrieve his signs. The road sergeant spotted what seemed to be an abandoned vehicle and began to run a routine check of the license plate. Just as the sergeant was calling in the plate to central dispatch, the newly elected Fenton approached the patrol vehicle and introduced himself to the sergeant. After exchanging pleasantries, Fenton returned to his vehicle.

Just as Fenton was pulling away, dispatch radioed the sergeant and advised him that the vehicle was registered to Walter Fenton of Brent Township. The sergeant was also told that there was an outstanding warrant from another jurisdiction for Fenton's arrest. The charge: none other than soliciting a prostitute. Perhaps exercising discretion, the sergeant chose not to chase the new trustee down and arrest him. Rather, he wrote a confidential note to the police chief and slid it in under the chief's office door for the morning. The next morning, with note in hand, the police chief approached Township Manager Matt Beckman with the news. Beckman asked how many people were aware of the warrant. The chief responded just he, the dispatcher, and the sergeant. He added that they all were being very discreet about it as they felt that Fenton was a likeable enough fellow. By that time, Beckman had some experience in matters of this nature, and he decided to try a new and different approach to this latest dalliance by an elected official. He decided in this case to approach the trustee directly without the involvement of the township supervisor.

Beckman called new Trustee Fenton at his tax accounting office in neighboring Chester Township. He congratulated him on his election and welcomed him to the township board. He asked Fenton to drop by the township offices after work. Fenton initially said that he was too busy, and suggested, "Perhaps tomorrow or the next day." Beckman told him that it concerned a rather important and urgent matter. He could picture Fenton's wheels turning, envisioning some important township matter that the manager needed to review with the new trustee. Fenton asked, "That important, is it?" After some persuasion, he agreed to meet with the township manager. Shortly after 5:00 PM, Fenton arrived at the offices and Beckman let him in the closed building. He led the trustee to his private conference room and closed the doors.

The smiling trustee made small talk about the election and the weather as the two of them became situated. It was obvious that Fenton still believed that this meeting was to discuss some important pressing matter in the township that the manager needed to bring him up to speed on. "So what is this big, major issue, Matt, that is so urgent?" he asked.

Clearing his throat, Beckman answered the question with a question. "Walt," he said, "are you aware that there is an outstanding warrant for your arrest?"

A puzzled and bewildered Fenton answered, "For what?"

"For soliciting a prostitute," was the reply.

With this, the new trustee's face quickly paled and he turned as white as a ghost. He swallowed hard, grabbed the edge of the table tightly to raise himself and went into the adjoining men's room and vomited. As he emerged, he still looked sickly and asked for a glass of water. As he sipped the water he told Beckman that it was "a very long time ago, and I was very drunk." Beckman assured Fenton that he did not need to know the details. He advised him that he just needed to get the matter cleared up in the city where it happened or he might not be so lucky if he were stopped by the police.

Rightfully so, Fenton was concerned that this incident would become public information and that his wife and family might find out. Beckman assured him that he and the police department would handle the situation discreetly. Fenton's secret was safe with Beckman. Not only did Fenton serve out his first term, he was reelected to a second term. The public never did know about his indiscretion and brush with the law.

Trustee Morgan

Township Manager Beckman placed a call to Trustee Carl Morgan's cell phone. "Carl," he asked "Did you have a run-in with the Concord police department over the weekend?"

Morgan replied, "Ah, what did you hear?"

"I heard that you were caught in a crack house with a 12-pack of beer under one arm and a prostitute under the other," Beckman told him. (By that time, Beckman had become an expert in dealing with elected officials who favor the services of the world's oldest profession.)

Morgan replied, "Ah, there is some truth to that but I can't talk to you on my cell phone about it. Can I meet you at O'Reilly's after work?" O'Reilly's was a popular watering hole in the township.

The manager and trustee met shortly after 5:00 PM. Beckman ordered a Miller Lite while Morgan surprisingly ordered a Diet Coke. He had been known to enjoy his beer, apparently a bit too much. Morgan, a respected architect whose services were in high demand, had only been on the township board for a year. He never missed a meeting until a period just before the incident that prompted Beckman's call to his cell phone. He had missed the past two meetings without as much as a call to the township offices. No one had heard from him and attempts to reach him were futile. He was incommunicado for nearly 6 weeks.

As they sat in O'Reilly's, Morgan explained his mysterious absence. "For the past 6 weeks, I have been at an in-house substance abuse rehabilitation center. I was not allowed visitors, nor could I make or receive telephone calls there. I have a drug and alcohol dependency and am trying to address this." That explained the Diet Coke. He told Beckman the following as to why he was found at a crack house with a hooker:

"In the rehab center they organize you into groups of eight. People from all walks of life are there . . . doctors, lawyers, engineers, and, yes, even prostitutes. As luck would have it, one was in my group and we got to know each other quite well during the 6 weeks I was there. As luck would also have it, the group that I was in selected me as the group leader.

"After 6 weeks of inpatient treatment, we then attend weekly outpatient treatment with the same group of people. These meetings are held from 6:00 PM to 9:00 PM every Friday night. The prostitute asked me if I could give her a ride home because her boyfriend had borrowed her car. I said sure. She directed me to an abandoned house in the inner city where she said she was meeting a friend. When we arrived, I got out of my car with her and went inside the house with her. I probably shouldn't have gone in, but I did. There were about eight other people there when all of the sudden, the house was surrounded by the police. They ordered all of us out of the house and searched us for drugs and weapons. I showed them my badge and told them I was an elected official from Brent Township and asked if they could show me some professional courtesy.

"After detaining us for about an hour and finding no drugs on me, they let me go. I do not know how you found out about all of this, but probably some of their cops told some of our cops."

He never did explain the 12-pack of beer. Beckman highly doubted that Morgan's rehab group met on Friday nights, let alone gathered afterwards to relax with beer. He doubted that this was part of the recovery program. Beckman thought, "That's his story and he's sticking to it." Morgan asked Manager Beckman what he should do. Did Beckman think that he should resign from the township board? The manager told Trustee Morgan that he might want to discuss it with the other board members individually, by telephone, or in person, as it was causing a bit of a stir in the community. Morgan did so and made a public announcement at the next township board meeting. He told the community that he had a substance abuse problem and was aggressively dealing with it. He assured them that he would not do anything in the future that would discredit the township. He apologized to the community for this recent indiscretion to which he attributed to poor judgment on his part. The community accepted his apology and most forgot all about it 3 years later when he ran successfully for a second term.

Summary

These three elected officials' behavior illustrate issues associated with the moral principles of ethical behavior. Two of the three compounded their moral principles violations by piling lies on top of them.

Questions

1. Are elected officials held to a different ethical standard depending who they are?

2. Why did Fenton and Morgan get away with their indiscretions when Curtis was forced to resign? Was it because Curtis was a blue collar worker and the other two were professionals?

3. If Township Manager Beckman had committed these ethical violations, what likely would have been his fate?

4. Was it ethical for Beckman to handle each of these in somewhat of a different fashion? Should he have gone to the township supervisor with the latter two as he had the first one?

5. Is it appropriate and/or ethical for elected officials to use their official position to escape responsibility or seek special treatment for their illegal activities as both Curtis and Morgan did?

6. Should the manager have recommended that Trustee Morgan resign because of his drug dependency?

Chapter 16

The Tax Is Illegal– Getting the Story Out

1. *Is it the TRUTH?*
2. *Is it FAIR to all concerned?*
3. *Will it build GOODWILL and better FRIENDSHIPS?*
4. *Will it be BENEFICIAL to all concerned?*

**—The "Four Way Test," written by Herbert J. Taylor,
adopted as creed of Rotary International, 1943**

Lunapark was an urbanized township. It used to have farms, but they were all gobbled up with housing developments. The only businesses were nonagricultural manufacturers, offices, and retail stores. A nearby city of Bedford had grown beyond its limits and most of Lunapark's residents worked in Bedford. When Lunapark was more rural, it did not have a police force, and its fire department was all volunteer and the equipment was quite basic.

With development came a full-time police force that grew to almost forty officers. The fire department maintained a volunteer structure, but there were eventually five full-time chiefs, and state-of-the-art fire engines and equipment gave the township the top rating for any force with volunteers. The developments of police and fire infrastructure had come with costs. In the 1950s, the state passed a law for urbanized townships allowing their boards to raise tax millages specifically for fire and police operations. These tax increases, according to the law, were to be levied only against real property, whether owned by residents or by businesses. However, the taxes were not to be levied against what was called business personal property. Business personal property consisted of things like equipment—typewriters, machines, etc.—and vehicles. The rationale for the discrepancy in how the taxes were applied may have related to the idea that a thief (object of police services) is unlikely to steal a large piece of business equipment, and similarly, such equipment is less likely to burn up in a fire. There was no tax on personal property in residences. The general township property tax levy was subject to strict state limitations and could only be raised by a vote of the people. This tax was to be applied to all property—real and business personal. Lunapark took advantage of the state law, and in 1952 the township board imposed a ten-mill tax for fire and police services. Ten mills equates to 1%, however, since the property was assessed at 50% of its value, in actuality it was a property tax of one half of 1% of the value of the property. For a house worth $200,000 and assessed at $100,000, the ten-mill tax amounted to $1,000 a year. The general township tax was gradually raised to fifteen mills as a result of various elections. The township also collected taxes for schools and for county services.

After the board (not the people) had voted in the levy for police and fire services, the township treasurer, with or without approval of other township officials, began sending out tax bills that assessed the township's full 25-mill levy on all assessed property—both real property and business personal property. And so the tax was collected. In fact, there were few factories and retail stores in the township at the time. As the new factories and businesses were built they received their tax bills and paid them—the same tax rate being applied to both their real and personal property. This went on for 27 years.

One Tuesday morning, Township Supervisor Tim Colwell was sitting in his office gazing out at the pretty flowers on the lawn in front of township hall. The phone rang. It was Mike Malone of the *Bedford Enterprise*. He bluntly said, "You know you are imposing illegal taxes on your businesses."

Colwell responded, "I am? Tell me about it."

"Yes, you are, and you have been doing it for 27 years, and we want to know what you're going to do about it," Malone said.

Tim said, "I better be filled in on the details before I answer a question like that. This is the first time I have heard such a thing."

Malone then described the state law, how the township board, not the voters, had passed the fire and police levies, and how the treasurer had been misapplying the tax to all property. Malone told Colwell that he must have been sleeping at the switch.

Colwell said, "Well, I've been in office 3 years, and you have been covering the township news for all 3 years, so maybe we have both been asleep, but I intend to respond. First I think I'll be calling the township attorney and some state officials up at the capitol. I promise I'll be back. By the way, did you dig this up all by yourself?"

Malone said, "I can't tell you my source, but it was a politically active citizen."

Colwell knew a pack of such citizens, one of whom was after his office. So be it. If they were doing wrong, they should correct their ways.

Colwell called the township attorney, who quickly checked the state law and agreed that the fire and police levy should apply only to real property. Colwell called the treasurer, and he said he'd been collecting taxes that way for 10 years, and he understood that was the way it was done before he had come to office. The clerk concurred. Colwell asked the clerk if he knew about the state law, and he just sort of smiled and said the issue had been discussed at a township association meeting once, but he let it pass. It was technically outside his job description, although he was responsible for putting the township budget together.

The idea hit the supervisor that some businesses had been overpaying their taxes for a long time, and they might be not only mad about it, but they might want their money back. He decided to call the state taxation office, division of local affairs. He also called the attorney general's office. The division of local affairs was very clear in its view, in fact its view had been tested in courts several times and it had been affirmed by the state supreme court. If a taxpayer paid taxes in excess of what was required by law, a rebate was in order only for taxes paid either in protest or taxes paid for services to be totally rendered in the future. As the last collection of taxes had been 6 months previously, and since no business taxpayers had protested the illegal tax when they had paid it, no business taxpayer could file a protest. The attorney general's office concurred in this judgment. Colwell was relieved over that. No money had to be paid back as a matter of law. However, there was a future to worry about. The attorney general's office told the supervisor that his knowledge of the situation thereafter rendered him liable if his government were to continue the practice in the future—meaning with its tax bills 6 months hence.

Colwell called Malone and shared his newfound information with the *Bedford Enterprise*. He also indicated that he would be working on a solution. And he told Malone that he wanted to make sure that the township was acting within the law in all cases. He indicated that the options included a cutback in police and fire services of about 15% or a comparable raise in the fire and police levy. These actions could be taken by the board, but at the moment he didn't care for either of them. Malone indicated that some other townships might be in the same situation, and the story was going to be big when it hit the newsstands. Considering the likely source of the story, Colwell was a bit concerned that the story could be slanted toward the notion of malfeasance and corruption and abuse of powers. Colwell did not think about it as a moral issue, because in his mind services were being rendered for the taxes received—after all, machinery can be destroyed in fires and thieves do steal typewriters. Nonetheless, he agreed that the law should be followed.

That Wednesday the Lunapark officials met with the officials of Liberty Township over a regional parks proposal. It was a chance to bring up the taxation matter. Colwell asked his neighboring supervisor if the tax issue was handled the same way in Liberty Township. It was. Colwell then asked the supervisor if he knew about the state law. He said, "Of course, we have known about it all the way along, but the businesses don't protest so we just take the money." The matter-of-fact answer sort of gave Colwell a jolt but he tried to conceal his amazement.

That evening he talked the matter over with the clerk and treasurer, and he floated the two options in front of them. The treasurer said, "Tim, you better check the 1952 law; I think it said we could only go to ten mills on the fire and police thing."

They grabbed the law book and sure enough that option was off the board. The option of cutting fire and police services 15% remained. They stared at each other and shook their heads. That was not what they wanted to do.

Then Colwell said, "Well, we could ask the citizens to vote on an increased general millage, and if it passed we could lower the fire and police millage a comparable amount. That way the citizens really wouldn't be paying any more, but the businesses would keep paying taxes on their business personal property."

The clerk said, "Boy that's a solution—just get the taxpayers to raise their taxes, so they don't have to pay any more in taxes." Colwell added that they could do an educational campaign and get business leaders to agree that they should all pay the same—their fair share. In fact, it would be a way to get businesses to praise the services they were getting from the police and fire department. All agreed that businesses were indeed happy with their services.

After a further review of state law, it was discovered that the board could, on its own, raise real estate taxes (but not personal business property taxes) two mills for specific capital equipment improvements for fire departments. So now the campaign could be couched in terms of, "Let's raise the general tax so we can remove the need to raise the special tax." In the end, the citizens would be paying a lower tax amount on their real estate property by approving the general tax increase.

Malone did not call on Thursday. Colwell feared that the story in the *Bedford Enterprise* could be devastating. There was no story on Thursday evening and no call from Malone on Friday. Colwell got the early Friday afternoon paper and there was no story. He thought defensively. They had a good story, they were going to propose a new tax so that citizens would pay less, but everyone would pay the same rate on all property. They just needed a vote of the people. But this was not going to be in Malone's story. Colwell called Malone's office. Malone was unavailable. Colwell decided to take the story to the public in his own words.

At 4:00 PM, he called his old friend, Martin Anthony, who was the news reporter at the public radio station. He described the situation, and Anthony was amazed. "Get your butt over here right now; we shall be live at five." Colwell jumped in his car and drove 12 miles to the station. Martin greeted him at the door and said, "We got the studio, we are on live at five." For 10 minutes they went through the details and the proposal that Colwell was making to correct the situation. The clerk and treasurer had agreed, and an agenda item to call a millage vote for the August election was ready to be acted upon. At 5:00 PM the whole story filled the airways on the public radio station. Anthony did a little salt-in-the-wound journalism as he kept saying it was a WBPR–Bedford Public Radio news exclusive. On Monday, at the township meeting, the citizens praised the officials for bringing their 27-year-long mistake to the public attention, and for enlisting the business community in making a correction so that all would be legal in the future. The meeting served as a campaign send-off for a positive vote to increase the general millage.

There was someone at the Monday township meeting who was not happy at all. Mike Malone had been put off by his paper because they thought the story was so big that it deserved front-page Sunday coverage. While Malone admitted the story was going to be quite negative, and it included quotations from angry citizens and the supervisor's opponent in the upcoming election, he was visibly angry. "This was my best story in months, and you took it to Anthony, you son of a bitch," he said to Colwell.

Instead of the front-page story on Sunday, there was a factual story about the issue on a back page of the Saturday edition of the *Bedford Enterprise*.

Supervisor Colwell genuinely liked Malone, so he smiled and said he understood, and in reverse circumstances he would feel the same. He asked, "Why, why, why had they held back on the story?" Colwell told Malone that he believed in a free press and appreciated his work even when it was critical, but that as a township officer he must also be concerned that the public saw the township government in a positive light, not just as a bunch of bumbling idiots who couldn't follow the law.

Malone was still angry. And as it turned out, his stories on the township and especially on Colwell took on a negative slant through the fall. Colwell was very satisfied when the millage referendum passed, and he announced that he was not going to seek another term in office.

The supervisor in Liberty Township had also put a general millage increase on the ballot, but without an effective campaign, the voters turned it down. As a result, he had either to cut police and fire services or to have the board impose a new tax just on real property without the approval of the people.

Questions

1. Should public officials honor information given to them by the press by not sharing it with other rival media?
2. How could Colwell have improved future relations with the *Bedford Enterprise*?
3. Should Colwell have given credit to Malone in his public radio interview?
4. Should Colwell have accepted blame for the past illegal collections of taxes? Should he have cast blame on his predecessors in office?
5. Are court decisions that illegal taxes collected in the past not be returned ethical? If not, should there be some statute of limitations on returns?

Chapter 17

Betty to the Rescue

"The highest form of treason: to do the right thing for the wrong reason."

—T.S. Eliot

Sometimes angels work behind the scenes in secret ways. Betty Mavis was an unsuspected angel for Supervisor Mark Armen of Glacier Hills Township. Glacier Hills was just north of the city of Westminister. Armen had been a political science professor at Ansell College in Westminister, but he was a resident of Glacier Hills, and when the opportunity present itself, he decided a tour of duty in public service was in order. He still had to get elected. Several students helped in his campaign and all were supportive. Particularly helpful was graduate student Paul Turwill. Turwill took the lead in getting together volunteers to knock on every door in Glacier Hills. He also talked residents into having signs on their lawn. In the true sense of the word, he was a go-getter. After long summer nights of campaigning, Armen and Turwill and those students who were over 21 would gather at the Knolls Tavern to discuss their activities. Betty Mavis often came along, usually with a textbook in hand, and always with a smile.

Armen told Turwill that he would help him get a job with the township if he were to be elected and a job opening was available. The election was a success, and as it happened, the previous, outgoing supervisor had a secretary who indicated she wished to resign when her boss left office. That created an opening for a secretary. Armen approached the township clerk, another elected official who served as personnel director. Armen was told that he could choose anyone he wished to be his secretary. He brought up the possibilities of having Turwill serve instead as his assistant, but with the understanding that Turwill and Armen would take care of all of the secretarial tasks of the supervisor's office. The clerk had no problem with that arrangement, and at the first meeting led by new Supervisor Mark Armen, the issue was placed in front of the full board, and it was discussed briefly. There was no opposition when it was established that Turwill could type and he had had some clerical work experience. Turwill was hired. He was able to continue with his master's degree program as all his remaining classes were in the evening. He agreed not to take any class on Monday night, as that was when the township board meetings were.

Political leaders often praise the patronage system. If an official is given the power to make an appointment untied to arms-length merit considerations and open competition, it is considered a plus. This is what Mark Armen had been teaching right out of the textbooks in his political personnel classes. He had his classes read *George Washington Plunkitt*,[1] which explained that the only way you can motivate staff is if you get to select them unhindered by rules and examinations. Patronage was the key to loyalty. When Armen the professor yielded to Armen the political leader, it didn't seem to work out that way at all. Turwill was a big mistake. He immediately took on a lazy air. He did not show respect to other members of the staff, mostly older women who, while a bit stern in demeanor, had efficiently taken care of township business over the previous 3 decades. Stern was the nature of most workers in the community of German immigrants—many of whom were recent immigrants. Turwill was a bit sloppy in his work. Armen had to have letters retyped, and after a while just took on the task of typing his letters by himself.

Armen was outgoing and liked to joke around with citizens and students alike. He was into jogging, and would tour the township streets in his running outfit two or three mornings a week. He actually used the running to look at sites for rezoning or other issues that had come up in meetings. It was a good way to keep in touch with the citizens. He would wave and smile at constituents and even stop to chat if the occasion called for it. Some of the solid citizens took offense at this style of activity. They were especially critical when they would phone the township and ask for the supervisor only to get Turwill to answer in a sarcastic way that the supervisor was out jogging.

Armen was very concerned when some of Turwill's college friends would stop by and have closed-door meetings with him. Armen also had an impression that Turwill and his friends would go behind the township hall and participate in recreational

---

[1]See Riordan, William. *Plunkitt of Tammany Hall*. Boston: Bedford Books of St. Martin's Press, 1994.

drug activity. Armen was well aware that many of the students on campus did drugs, and he had seen Turwill smoking on occasion. The township hall was not the place, and working hours were not the time.

A patronage appointee cannot be easily fired. This is especially the case if he or she earned the job through hard political work. This is the case when someone won an appointment through the recommendation of a close friend. A patronage appointee who knows this may use this. The patronage appointee may take on a feeling that he already paid his dues for the job and he doesn't have to work as hard as others for their pay. Such was the case with Turwill. Armen pondered solutions, and he knew that any direct action would have costs in friendships on campus, and in respect from his township colleagues who had gone along with his judgment when Turwill was hired. The solution to the problem of Turwill was not easy. Armen's first thought was to move him to some work outside of the township hall. Armen did let Turwill know that he could not defend him if anyone else saw him smoking marijuana about the premises, and Turwill seemed to understand the warning.

Armen thought about putting Turwill with the township work crews, but that was mostly manual labor, and Armen was not going to make Turwill a supervisor of work crews—where the workers were more skilled than he was. Fortunately the township received a neighborhood development grant for a poor area near the river—Riverdale. The grant entailed hiring crews to clean up the streets, paint houses, and conduct recreational programs. Armen put Turwill in charge of organizing teams to go to the Riverdale area and to work with them. While Turwill thought the work was a bit demeaning, he thought it was less boring that being at township hall all day. He seemed to be doing a satisfactory job in Riverdale. Armen only worried about the fall—in 2 months the Riverdale project would be over—then he would have the Turwill project on his hands again.

Ah! The day of miracles. One day in August, Turwill came into Armen's office with a big smile and announced that there was an opening for an assistant public works director in the city of Westminister, and the pay was 40% higher than his current salary. He asked if he should apply.

Armen put on his professor's hat for a moment and said, "Paul, you know you are welcome here. I owe you this; I know I wouldn't be here without your work. But the job you have here has to be considered temporary—I am here on a 2-year term; you know my job here is temporary too. You do not have a career job here; there is no career ladder. Westminister is a big city, a post like assistant public works director can have a career ladder. And I can't raise your salary. Believe me, I know I owe you, and I know you can work hard, and I'll let the people in Westminister know you are a good student and you can work hard. My professorial advice is simply 'go for it.'"

Armen made a few inquiries about the position in Westminister, and he found that they wanted a person with a master's degree and experience, and that they were conducting a national search. His brief moments of thinking that the "Paul problem" was being solved ended. On the other hand, maybe his talk with Turwill could encourage him to look for other jobs, too. But hopes dashed can be hopes revived. Two days later Turwill told the supervisor that he had made the list of ten finalists for the job at Westminister. Armen was indeed a bit dumbfounded.

The next week Turwill was invited for a personal interview. He reported back to Armen with another smile on his face. He had been the first candidate interviewed, because they were talking to people in the local area first. He related that the interview had gone extremely well. In the course of discussions about work experience Turwill had told the Westminister director of public works that he had worked on sidewalk construction crews during summers of his college years. The director asked where, and Turwill replied in Geddes, where he grew up. Geddes was a town of 10,000, forty miles to the west of Glacier Hills.

"You grew up in Geddes?" the director had exclaimed. "So did I. Turwill, your name is? Is that right?"

"Yes, Paul Turwill."

The director asked, "Do you know Tom Turwill?"

"Of course," Turwill replied. "That's my father."

"I can't believe it. Your father, wow! You must be that little kid he brought to the class picnics," the director said. "Your father was my best buddy all though school. The stories I won't tell you, wow!"

And so went the interview. The director said he would call Turwill in a few days.

The next day the director called Mark Armen. Armen gave Turwill a toned-down good recommendation, but the director sensed something. He asked, "You're not trying to get rid of him are you?"

Without giving a direct answer, Supervisor Armen repeated the essence of his conversation with Turwill. "I am also Paul's professor at the college, and I have to reflect on what the job here means and what your job would mean for his career. You are offering a professional public administration post with career opportunities. His job here is simply more limited. He is certainly welcome to stay here, but you are presenting a real professional opportunity and he is capable of taking advantage of it and doing a good job."

Armen worried that his line of bull might not be effective, but he let it rest, and the director thanked him for his views on Turwill. Turwill got the job.

Armen dropped into the Knolls a few weeks later and Betty Mavis strolled in, books in hand. He asked her how the term was going. She said, "This internship and one more class and I've got my degree."

"Hey, great, tell me about your internship," Armen said.

Mavis said, "You should know about my internship, you helped set it up last fall."

Armen sort of remembered and said, "Something to do with personnel, at the county."

"Right on personnel, but it is the personnel department with the city of Westminister, and let me tell you, I saved your friend Paul's butt, too."

Armen inquired as to how she had done that.

Mavis related that the applicants for the assistant public works director were on her desk, and a screening committee had selected ten for interviews. Turwill's application was in the pile of rejected applications. Mavis said she simply took out the bottom application from the pile of ten and placed Turwill's into the second spot. Evidently, the director just grabbed the pile of ten and sorted out the locals, and Turwill was the first one to get an interview call. Mavis heard he had gotten the job, but she hadn't told anyone how he got the interview. Turwill told her that she had really saved him. She said she thought so because Turwill was always complaining about his township job.

Armen had not thought about Mavis's graduation, and Mavis had not brought up the subject. But Armen knew she was a waitress at a nice restaurant, the Great Lakes Steakhouse. Armen went into the tavern the week after graduation, and Mavis was there again. This time she was direct.

"Hey, Professor, when you going to take care of me? When do I get a job?"

Armen said, "O.K. Right now, this is your job interview."

They went though her courses, the jobs she had held, and her skill levels.

Armen said, "Look, I never filled Paul Turwill's job, and I told the clerk I really didn't need an assistant, but I know we have a backlog of clerical work, and we could use some organization. You come in tomorrow, and we'll discuss your job with the clerk."

The next day Mavis was hired. Armen returned to teaching when his 2-year term ended. Mavis's new job was a clerical job, but over the next 25 years she grew her position into a professional position. The word in township hall was that she made the place work. Indeed she was even recognized by the Greater Westminister Women's Club as "Professional Woman of the Year."

Rethinking patronage—sometimes it can work out O.K.

Questions

1. Patronage involves basic ethical questions. Was it proper for Armen to hire Turwill in the first place? There was certainly more qualified office staff available.

2. What could Armen have done to let Turwill know that his position with the township involved serious work?

3. Shouldn't Armen have had some clues about how Turwill might act in the township office situations? Wouldn't he have been familiar with his character? Did he do a disservice to Turwill by not carefully determining (and telling him) his specific job duties, and specific expectations for on-the-job work?

4. Was the director of public works skirting his job when he let friendships lead him to hire Turwill? Was he just lazy and wanting to avoid having to conduct a large number of interviews?

5. Was Mavis's action unethical? Was it illegal?

6. Should Supervisor Armen have rewarded Mavis with a job?

7. What would have been the consequences if Armen had simply told Turwill, "You can't work here anymore"?

Chapter 18

Not Following the Letter of the Law Is Best Sometimes

"Be not too moral, you may cheat yourself out of much life so. Aim above morality. Be not simply good, be good for something."

—Henry David Thoreau

Titan Autoworks had been a mainstay industry in Cambridge for over 50 years. Its pride and joy was the Titan, a comfortable, four-door limousine with expansive interior room, great trunk space, and sturdy frame work. The Titan could ride six or seven in semiluxury while carrying all their luggage. It could take the bumps and potholes of the highways and byways of America with low maintenance needs. For these reasons, taxicab companies not only in the United States but around the world featured fleets of Titans, affectionately known as the black and white cabbies.

There was only one problem with the Titan, which had an appearance similar to a classic BMW. The Titan got about 7 miles per gallon of fuel. This was a small problem until 1973, when the gas crunch hit, and fuel prices went from 25¢ a gallon to over a dollar. Orders for new Titans decreased dramatically, and car production at the Cambridge plant fizzled. The leaders at Titan toyed with entering a joint agreement with Toyota to make a fuel-efficient smaller cab, but the leaders had known success for too many years with their larger product. It was not in their hearts to change. By the end of the decade, they were turning out fewer than 100 cars a year, and their assembly lines had been converted so that they could make spare panels for various General Motors and Ford models of cars. Their doors remained open, but they couldn't say much more.

The Cambridge mayor, George Harris, operated as both the chief executive of his government and the official property assessor. After he was elected, he studied diligently for his assessor examinations. He attended courses at the local community college, and he worked hard to prepare for his tests. First he received a high pass on the residential property examination, and 2 months later he received a very high pass on his commercial property assessment examination. He was fully certified as an assessor for all properties in the city by the time he was sworn in to office. While he was the official assessor, his many other duties did not allow him much—if any— time to perform the day-to-day duties of property assessment. Those duties were left to Assistant Assessor Jim Gould, who was also fully certified. While political work is rarely routine, property assessment is, and Gould was very good at his job. He knew the routine and he loved his job. He could justify in detail exactly why one property was assessed at one level and another at another level. He knew the formulas and he applied them according to the letter of the law. Whenever he had an idea he wanted to discuss with Harris, Harris was so impressed that he could hardly find an opening for a suggestion or two.

Titan Autoworks was one of the most important taxpayers in Cambridge. Its annual property tax bill exceeded $120,000. In the previous year, its buildings and equipment had been assessed as having a value of $4 million.

Harris had learned about the systems used for assessment in his courses. Residential homes were measured for square footage and various amenities. These factors were then compared with sales records for similar homes in a sector of the city. As sales of homes were ongoing, a record of sales would guide annual additions to the value of the houses across the board within a city sector. Of course, if sale prices declined, property assessments would decline. Another system was used for retail, rental, and office property—the income approach. For, instance, bottom line profits might be multiplied by a factor of ten, the assumption being that the property returned 10% on its capital investment. Industrial properties were evaluated on a cost-to-replace basis. The original construction costs would be factored into a value using inflation and appropriate depreciation figures. For annualized values of both income approach and cost basis evaluations, the assessor would typically consult with the state business services office and receive a figure (percentage) indicating the growth (or decline) of business activity for a town or city. The percentage would be added to the previous year's assessment along with the value of any recent additions and improvements. In all cases—for homes and businesses—the assessed value for taxation was one half of the actual cost.

The state indicated to Harris and Gould that business activity had increased 10% in actual dollar value in the city of Cambridge over the previous year. Therefore, they agreed that the value of business and industrial properties would be assessed

10% higher than the previous year, in addition to any improvement costs. Notices of new assessments were sent to all the property owners.

The previous year, Titan's properties had been assessed with the replacement cost method specified in the state law as being worth an actual $4 million. Hence for taxation purposes, the assessed value was $2 million (50%) of actual value. The notice that Titan company controller Peter Hill received said that Titan's new assessment was $2.2 million. Hill had accepted the previous year's assessment without complaint, but he decided to protest. The assessment was just too high, and Titan was not going to stand for it.

Hill had worked closely with assessor Gould over the previous years as they would go over equipment purchase lists and invoices from companies constructing additions to their buildings. So they were on friendly terms with each other. But Hill's phone call to Gould had an edge to it. "Jim," he said, "we just can't pay the higher taxes; we are going to have to protest our assessment."

Jim said, "O.K., let's get together and talk. Your place or mine?"

They agreed to meet at city hall so that Mayor Harris could join the conversation if he desired. The three sat down together. Harris took the lead. "Peter, we want to work with you any way we can. I guess you think the increase was a bit much. It was what the state told us was appropriate considering our business growth, but what say you? A 5% increase, perhaps?"

"Look, I'm not here to talk about any 5 or 10% increase. The assessment is just plain too much. We want it lowered by half to one million," Hill said.

"But, Peter," Jim replied, "Last year you accepted a $2 million assessment without protest. That's a matter of record. We have followed all the provisions in the state law on this one. You can't win."

"Mayor Harris, Jim, we are going to fight you on this one," Hill told them. "I have a letter here that our president sent to corporate counsel authorizing him to negotiate a $1 million assessment or to protest the assessment in court. And you can see in the letter that we are prepared to go all the way to the state supreme court if we have to."

Harris and Gould were stunned. This was something right out of left field. But they were cordial. Hill told them that they could come over and talk with the president to get the view straight from the horse's mouth, as it were. The assessors indicated that they might be having that conversation soon.

After Hill left, Harris and Gould called Bill Stout, the city attorney, and they had a good sit-down conversation. Stout indicated that he could not figure out how Titan could possibly think it could win the case. But he was also realistic. He said, "Look at it this way. They want their assessment lowered from what it is now by $1 million. At our sixty mill tax rate, they are seeking to avoid $60,000 in taxes that they willingly paid last year. No court will buy that. But we have to be careful. You know the city does not get all of that tax money—not by a long shot. Sixty per cent, or $36,000, goes to the school district, and the county and special districts get another 25%, or $15,000. The city gets only 15%, or $9,000.

"That's the game we are playing. Yet it is our responsibility to do the assessments, and to collect the taxes, and here as in this matter, to defend—in court if we have to—our taxation process. We can defend it—open and shut case as I see it, but you know, it costs just about $10,000 to get a case through the state supreme court. Something to think about. But hey, my legal advice, we will be winners in court." Harris related to Stout that it seemed the party with the most at stake was the school district. Fairness would dictate that they help with the legal costs. Stout agreed that that would be fair, but they were dealing with politics and the law, and it was the city's duty to carry the matter to court.

Mayor Harris checked the law, and everything Stout said was correct, nonetheless in the interest of fairness, he thought he would call his old friend Steve Pennington, the superintendent of schools.

Pennington bought into Harris's arguments all the way. In fact, he said, "I truly think we ought to help, and I wish we could help. But," he added, "There is a state law, and if I used school funds for this, I could be thrown out of my position, and maybe even thrown in jail. The law is clear. I'd love to help you, brother, but they won't let me vote. I don't want to be kidding about this. I really do hope you win this one. Sorry."

Harris conveyed the response to both Gould and Stout. Gould said that he had received another call from Hill, and that they had set up a meeting with the Titan president, and that Hill really wanted to work things out peacefully without the matter having to go to court. Harris agreed to attend.

The president was very cordial. He reminded Harris that in previous years when the city had conducted the Cambridge 10-K road race, that Titan not only provided a symbolic pace car, but that they had also made a $500 contribution for prizes. He reminded Harris that they had declined to participate in this year's race and he reminded him why. He had told Harris that they had had no profits this year and that the controller had advised him to dispense with his discretionary fund. Indeed, the president said that if the meeting were held a year earlier, they would be having lunch at the Cambridge Country Club. The reality of it was that the company was going under. When they saw the notice of the new property tax assessment, it was more than the writing on the wall. If they couldn't cut taxes drastically and immediately, he indicated that their doors would be closed by the end of the year. He said he did not want to see that happen, nor did his 600 workers. Harris sympathized, but he added that they were bound by the letter of the tax law and that hardship cases had to be presented to a state board. The president indicated that an appeal of hardship would be a public matter and the publicity would be very harmful to all aspects of Titan's current operations—to its relationships with its suppliers, to its contract customers at General Motors and Ford, and to its public image generally. Titan wanted a township tax break immediately via a cut of its assessment by one half. Harris told the president that he wished he could find a way to do just that legally, but that he was bound by the law.

The president asked Hill to tell Harris and Gould what they will be up against if they went to court. Hill said, "I know you believe you have the law 100% on your side, and that you are certain you will win a court case. But we will present a case too. We think a local judge and justices of the supreme court will be sympathetic to our desire to keep 600 local residents employed. But we will not be pleading for sympathy alone. You might suspect that we are in the market to sell our operations. Unfortunately, if that happens, it will be essentially what you would call a fire sale. There is not much demand for a used automobile plant these days—maybe in Japan, but not in the U.S.A. We hired the most recognized industrial appraiser in the land—you know them, Bernick and Suttons of Chicago. They said that the best we could hope to receive for our business was the value of our plant buildings and the land they are on. They put the appraised value if the buildings were to be sold at $1.8 million. So you see, if we agree to a $1 million assessment, we are giving you more than you deserve. Bernick and Suttons gave us a value based upon the market sales approach. We know factories are supposed to be assessed on the replacement cost approach, but if you read the law closely, it does not mandate that a specific approach to assessments be made in every case, and there is room in the law to make a reasonable claim for using another assessment approach. We just want you to think about this as you make a decision. We have enjoyed our relationship with the township over the years; let's keep it good, dare I say, to the end."

Harris, Gould, Hill, and the president shook hands, and Harris said that he would talk with Hill the next day.

Hill and Gould discussed the matter with attorney Stout, and they agreed that they could cut the assessment to $900,000. They would let Hill know immediately, but they would also request that they have a copy of the Bernick and Suttons report. Their assessment cut would be done quietly without any public announcement. However, the cut would have to be a matter of public record for anyone who wanted to dig it out. The city government simply wanted to have a record from which it could legally defend an action that was quite divergent from precedence.

Other factory-based businesses in the city were doing fairly well considering the general economic climate, and as long as they were in the black ink territory, they would not be upset with the action taken toward Titan Autoworks.

Titan was able to weather a few more storms as it remained open for the remaining year of Mayor Harris's term in office. However, the year after Harris left office, the business closed down permanently. No one purchased the building, and all the employees lost their jobs.

Questions

1. Were Harris and Gould acting properly by even thinking of going to court over the Titan assessment dispute?

2. Was it a bad precedent to cut the assessment on basically humanitarian grounds, when such action should have properly been taken by a state board?

3. Should the city have issued a press statement to the public regarding the action they were taking?

4. Should the city have invited the school district into the meetings with Hill and the president of Titan Autoworks?

5. What should Harris and Gould have done if a successful manufacturer in the city demanded that the market sales approach be used in assessing its property?

Chapter 19

Because of Good Intergovernmental Relations, Some Things Could Be Buried Quickly

"All that is necessary for the triumph of evil is that good men do nothing."

—Edmund Burke

The Greater Grand River School District decided to build its new high school on a parcel of land within Eastman Township. It was to be a three-story structure. As the parcel of land abutted the dividing line between Eastman Township and the much larger city of Grand River, the school district made a concerted effort to have the land annexed to the city. The school officials claimed that they needed the higher quality police and fire services of the city.

Although the parcel of land was not subject to taxation, the township challenged the action, and Eastman won a special court order enjoining an annexation action by the city. The court (judge) recognized that while the township fire services were based upon volunteers serving out of a station with an on-duty chief, the station in this case was only 1 mile from the school. On the other hand, the city fire station serving the area was over 6 miles away. The township fire station also served as a substation for its full-time police force. The township and the city shared a common water and sanitation sewer district, so these services never were at issue. The judge's decision was made easier when the township made a binding commitment to purchase a hook and ladder fire truck that could reach the top of the new school structure.

The school district was content with the decision, and they pledged not to appeal the ruling to a higher court. In actuality, the effort at annexation was made to appease several school trustees who represented more affluent city areas, and, in effect, considered the formerly rural township to be quite inferior in terms of services. The reality was that school district managers had been very satisfied in its relations with Eastman Township, 90% of whose residents lived in the school district. The Greater Grand River School District had six schools in the township, the new high school, a middle school, and six elementary schools. They had no complaints about the police and fire services. Indeed, it was township police chief Bob Ryland who was a bit testy when he learned that a school principal had not called the police when it was discovered that two children brought guns to school. However, when a call came from any school to the police, it received top priority in order of response. The township police were also regularly on the scene to monitor traffic safety before and after school.

The township performed one very critical task on behalf of the school district. The township assessed the value of property that was in the township and the school district, and they issued tax bills to the township residents—bills that covered township, county, water district, and school taxes. The township also collected the taxes, and the township treasurer promptly transferred the school tax money to the treasurer of the school district. The township never even thought about playing games with the money. While the township passed tax money out to other entities, they were also the recipient of 25% of the sales tax revenues that the state collected in the township. This money first went to the state treasury, and then it was transferred to the township. Without warning or notice the state decided one day that it would send the money to local governments quarterly rather than monthly—although most had already figured their budget spending plans on the basis of monthly infusions of sales tax money. Even then, the checks would often come up to a week late. The cash-strapped state was playing an old public finance game of holding on to someone else's dollar for as long as it could in order to maximize its bank interest. When money came late from the state, it never came with interest. The township transferred school district tax collections to the school district immediately as received into an account that the township could continue to monitor, but was also immediately accessible by the school district. If a taxpayer paid taxes early, the school district received the full advantage of the early payment, including any extra interest the money received while being held in a bank account. The school district was openly appreciative of the fact that the township never remotely considered playing games with its money.

The Eastman Township officials, led by Supervisor Curtis Palmer, Clerk Len Manchester, and Treasurer Don Voorhies, had also pledged that the bulk of the year's federal neighborhood development funds would go to support housing rehabilitation and recreation programs revolving about an elementary school that served the poorest children in the Greater Grand River School District. The programs were based at the local school.

Overall, most observers found that relationships between the township government and the school district were very good. They were tested during the second year of Curtis Palmer's term of office as supervisor of Eastman Township.

Palmer got along very well with Manchester and Voorhies. All were elected at large, while five council members were elected from wards. All eight served together as the legislative board of the township, with Palmer being chairman of the board. The board had to approve all expenditures made by the township. All purchases had to be presented as appropriation agenda items for action by the entire board.

Treasurer Voorhies was in his final term of office. He was approaching his 70th birthday. He had served the township well for over 25 years, 10 as a board member, and nearly 16 as treasurer. He had been an accountant before becoming township treasurer. Clerk Manchester was the main spark plug who kept the township government running. He had been the owner of a retail store before selling it to his brother and taking over as clerk the decade before. Supervisor Palmer was on leave from a position as a school teacher.

Palmer and Manchester were very respectful and sympathetic toward Voorhies's concern that the township-owned cemetery was nearly filled up. It was the only cemetery in the township. Voorhies had always expressed the desire that he and his wife could rest always near their friends and family in Eastman Township.

One day Voorhies came into Manchester's office with a look of happiness and excitement on his face. He said, "Call Palmer in here now." When Palmer arrived, Voorhies read an announcement he had just received from the school district. The school district was having a surplus land sale. He said, "You know, they have a parcel of land that is right next to my church on Mallard Road. It's the land that goes right up to the woods. That would be a dandy place for a cemetery."

Palmer and Manchester agreed. Voorhies told them that they would have to act quickly. He said the notice of the sale was dated 3 days before, but it just came in the mail. It said the sale would be an auction of sealed bids, and they had to be submitted by the next day. The township board was not meeting until the next Tuesday evening. Manchester said he would send the assessor out to measure the parcel and judge its other possible uses and to put a value on it based upon values of other land in the immediate area.

The assessor came back and said if he had to assess the land he would say it had a market value of $20,000. The supervisor, clerk, and treasurer talked it over and agreed that it would be safe to submit a bid for $18,000, which they did. It turned out that they did bid a bit high as only one other party wanted the land, and he was willing to pay only $12,000. But they wanted it, and they needed it, and they got it. The township was almost the owner of a parcel of land where it could build a cemetery, near a church, in the shade of adjacent woods.

There was one little detail that the three had to finesse. The board had not approved the purchase, and it was not meeting for 4 days. That was good because the open meetings law required 3 days' notice for an agenda item. The item of discussing new lands for a cemetery and taking appropriate action was put on the agenda.

The item was at the bottom of the agenda, as it was the last item added. The board sat through $2^{1}/_{2}$ hours of discussion about a liquor license renewal and three minor zoning changes that were uncontested but had to be subjected to a review of plans and charts presented by attorneys.

When the issue of a cemetery came up, all were in a conciliatory mood. Palmer said he and the clerk, Manchester, had been thinking that it was time to explore the cemetery situation in the township. All the board members and the treasurer nodded approval. Palmer then said that they were going to search for a parcel of land in the township, and they were going to start with surplus lands available from the school district. Several of the parcels looked like they had possibilities. They would like to have prior approval to consider making bids on the lands. Again, there were nods of approval.

Palmer was about to request a motion to vote on the matter, when council member Thad Van Dusen, who was also a member of Treasurer Voorhies's church, said, "I sure hope you are not thinking about that parcel of school land up on Mallard Road next to my church." Palmer said that was one of the parcels on the list, so he would be happy to have Thad's opinion about it.

Board member Van Dusen offered that the township would certainly not want to consider that piece of land for a cemetery. He suggested that it had so many rocks in it that a grave digger could devote his entire career to getting ready for one funeral and burial. Palmer thanked him for his comments, and said they would certainly be concerned about soil conditions. Palmer paused and said that perhaps they could move to new business. There being none, he asked for a motion for adjournment.

After appropriate niceties that went along with the close of each township meeting, Palmer winked at Manchester, Manchester whispered to Voorhies, and the three retreated for a quick moment in private reflection. Palmer suggested sending the maintenance crew over to the land first thing in the morning. All agreed. They would meet again when the crew returned. And so it was as Van Dusen had told them. The crew said they couldn't get a shovel fully into the soil anywhere before it hit a rock. The land simply could not be used as a cemetery.

The three officials sat in disbelief shaking their heads. Then Manchester said, "Look, School Superintendent Guinn is my neighbor. We did a barbeque at his house last week. He knows we look after the interests of the schools. I'll put the egg on my face. We got to get out of this."

And so with years of goodwill in his briefcase, Manchester carried the news to the school district that the township had to back down on a deal that they had made in good faith. Manchester reported back that he really felt small, but that the superintendent and his property manager, scowled and then sort of smiled. They let Manchester know that they would have land sales in the future, and they made it clear that the township owed them one.

Manchester shook their hands and agreed. "You are 100% right on that." The school officials also said they would not report any notice of the township's bid, that they would just disregard it and give the other bidder the option to buy the land if he wanted it.

When Manchester reported back to Palmer and Voorhies, the three agreed that they didn't have to post a notice to the public on their actions, either. From that day until the day Voorhies left office in retirement and Palmer returned to teaching, not a word of the matter came up at township hall.

Questions

1. While it was a violation of township purchasing rules to make a bid on land without prior approval, was it morally wrong to do so, given an accepted view that they needed land for the purpose indicated?

2. Was it a violation of law to make the bid, in that the actual purchase would have to follow formal action by the township board?

3. Should Palmer have revealed the actions that he, Manchester, and Voorhies (all township officers) had taken to other board members?

4. Should the school district have been aware that the township wanted the land for a cemetery, and that the land did not have proper soil to be a cemetery? If school officials knew so, was it ethical for them to have honored the township bid for the land?

5. Should the school officials have supported the township in its embarrassing moment by allowing the matter to be private and to strike the official bid of the township from their public records?

6. Was this case anything like the Louisiana Purchase? President Jefferson sent an envoy to France to discuss the purchase of the port of New Orleans. The envoy returned to Jefferson telling him he had committed the United States to the purchase of the whole Louisiana Territory for over $15 million. This turned out to be one of the greatest purchases in U.S. history. Was it an immoral action?

7. Was the Louisiana Purchase illegal? Consider that Jefferson took the matter to Congress and Congress actually appropriated the $15 million for the purchase in the proper manner, albeit a commitment had been made before.

Chapter 20

The Rarest of the Rare

"Ethics, too, are nothing but reverence for life. This is what gives me the fundamental principle of morality, namely, that good consists in maintaining, promoting, and enhancing life and that destroying, injuring, and limiting life are evil."

—Albert Schweitzer

Elmberg is a midsize city located in the suburbs of a major metropolitan area in the Southeast. It is predominantly residential, but it has a spattering of commercial and light industrial areas. Most of the post–World War II homes are small bungalows set on small lots. Elmbergers, as they kiddingly call themselves, are mostly middle class, blue collar workers. Despite its presence in a major metropolis, it has a small-town feel and it seems that everybody knows everybody.

Its city manager, Rob Hall, had been at the helm, so to speak, for over 20 years, almost unheard of in the field. One particularly warm summer evening, Rob did what he enjoyed most, sitting on his patio and reading to relax. For years, Rob read true crime books. Not novels, not fiction, but crime books about real murderers, real victims, and real events. As soon as he would put one down he would start another one. He would go through one, sometimes two of these a month. On summer vacations it would not be unusual for him to read three of these true crime dramas in

2 weeks. His favorite author was Ann Rule, a former Seattle police officer turned writer.

"I think that you are a frustrated cop," his wife would often say.

"No," he would comment, "I just think they are like a long newspaper article about something a community is dealing with." Despite her lighthearted criticisms, she enjoyed hearing the stories as Rob read his books. And she was a fan as much as he was of true crime television shows such as *48 Hours, City Confidential,* and *Forensic Files.*

Mark White worked at the city's wastewater treatment plant. He had been with the city for about 7 years when his daughter, Erin, was struck with an illness that prevented her from attending school. Mark was somewhat of a marginal employee, at best, and he had been disciplined several times for tardiness, poor work habits, and his violent outbursts when he lost his temper. It would be fair to say that he was a problem employee.

Erin White was a student at Coolidge Elementary School. A March 6th article in the *Elmberg News* had featured Erin and her family. According to the article, 10-year-old Erin had many allergies and asthma. After a November 5th visit to her allergist and a new prescription, she seemed to be doing better, but her mother and family spokesperson, Gail White, said that by the end of November Erin was "sicker than a dog."

The article went on to say that tests at Holy Cross Hospital indicated a mass and polyps had grown on Erin's sinuses, broken the bone in the orbital cavity, and attached to the right eye muscle. Gail White explained that two operations were performed to remove the mass and polyps from Erin's sinus cavity, and Erin's heart rate increased and her asthma flared up. A lung biopsy at Amalgamated Hospitals showed that Erin had a nodule near her heart. According to White, additional surgery would be required when Erin was stronger. She was quoted as saying, "Erin is not a statistic and is not in any book."

Gail White also said that Erin was unable to attend school because of a PICC[1] line inserted in her arm, so a tutor from Coolidge visited her twice a week. Gail White also explained that Erin suffered blurred vision in her right eye, so Gail read most of Erin's assignments to her to avoid undue eyestrain.

In the article, Gail White thanked the soccer association and the school for helping the family by providing meals and giving Erin's two brothers rides to soccer while the Whites took Erin to various doctor's appointments. Coolidge faculty members and parents of Coolidge students took up a collection to donate money to help the Whites with Erin's medical expenses. Gail White also thanked her friends for kidnapping her and taking her out for drinks.

---

[1] PICC stands for peripherally inserted central catheter. It is needle-like and usually inserted in the patient's arm with one or more short tubings left exposed. Lines can be left in place for weeks at a time to administer intravenous fluids and medications without the need to stick the patient every time.

When City Manager Hall read the *Elmberg News* account of White's daughter's illness, he determined this to be a triggering event under the federal Family Medical Leave Act, more commonly referred to in the vernacular as the FMLA.[2] As such, his office provided Mark White with a copy of the city's FLMA policy, as well as the necessary forms to be completed if he wished to apply for leave.

In late July, about 5 months after the first article about 10-year-old Erin White's illness, Nora Monk of the *Elmberg News* wrote a second, follow-up article.

In the second article, Gail White was again the family spokesperson. Mrs. White said that the family had recently returned from a 12-day stay in Memphis, where Erin was hospitalized at St. Jude Children's Research Hospital. Mrs. White explained that Erin had been diagnosed with Warner's disease,[3] a condition that eats away at the lung tissue and raises the enzyme levels in both the kidneys and liver. She indicated that Erin was the 501st person to be diagnosed with the "rarest of the rare" disease. "There is no reason for the disease," she told the reporter. "It is set off by an infection." She elaborated that Erin's sinusitis might have been the triggering infection. Gail White explained that the disease caused tumorlike nodules on both of Erin's lungs, which could not be removed surgically.

Gail White continued that Erin would be treated with cyclophosphamide, and the side effects were expected to cause Erin to vomit and lose weight and hair. Some of the treatments would be done in Elmberg, but more travel to Memphis would be required. Although the cyclophosphamide would not cure the disease, the Whites hoped for a remission.

The article said that family friends were in the initial stages of planning and fundraising activities.

As word of Erin's incurable disease spread throughout Elmberg, the community's sympathies and generosity poured in. Mark and Gail White established the Erin Anne White Foundation, complete with a tax identification number, for family, friends, and neighbors to contribute to to offset the family's mounting medical bills. They told potential contributors that their contributions were tax deductible. That fall, they, along with the Elmberg Soccer Association, scheduled a spaghetti dinner and silent auction benefit to raise funds. A flyer from the foundation was prepared and distributed to prospective contributors to the silent auction, explaining that the purpose of the auction was to help the Whites defray Erin's mounting medical costs, and stating that donations would be tax deductible.

A similar flyer for the event was being widely distributed by the soccer association. Friends and supporters placed canisters at restaurants, barber shops, and beauty

---

[2] The Family Medical Leave Act was enacted by the U.S. Congress in 1993. It allows eligible employees to take off up to 12 weeks of work, unpaid, in any 12-month period for the birth or adoption of a child, to care for a family member, or if the employee has a serious health condition.

[3] The name of the disease has been changed for this chapter.

parlors, including the one that Gail and her daughter frequented. Proceeds benefited the Erin Anne White Foundation.

This is truly a sad story . . . a very sad one indeed. The story of a dying 10-year old girl would tug at anyone's heart strings. Mounting medical bills. A growing medical crisis. An incurable disease. Who could not feel deep sorrow for Erin and her family?

It would be even sadder so if it were true, but it was *not*! Ten-year-old Erin might very well die all right. But it would not be from an incurable disease, but potentially at the hands of her mother.

Elmberg City Manager Rob Hall was, as usual after work, sitting on his patio near his small koi pond enjoying the warm July evening. His wife, Karen, brought out to him the latest edition of the *Elmberg News*. As she handed it to him she said, "There is a follow-up article on your employee's little girl that is so sick. I feel so sorry for her and her family. I don't know if I ever told you this, but Gail White goes to the same hairdresser as Sue [their 30-year-old daughter] and I go to . . . Carol Cook. When I was there yesterday, Carol told me that Gail White is a regular customer as well, though I've never met her. Apparently Mrs. White goes there every 2 weeks to have her hair and nails done and spends about $125 each time, even though Carol says she won't accept it given their financial strapping. But Gail insists on paying and does so each time including a generous tip. Carol told me about the silent auction that they are having to raise funds for the White family and I offered to donate one of my handmade ceramics."

"That was very generous and thoughtful of you," Rob told her. As he read this most recent article, something did not strike him right. Incurable disease? The rarest of the rare? Vomiting . . . loss of weight . . . loss of hair? The 501st patient? It almost sounded like she was bragging. It just did not make sense to him. And most notably absent from the article was any quote from any doctor. They were all quotes from the mother. When he finished reading the article he looked up and asked his wife, "Remember a couple of summers ago I read those two true crime books about mothers who killed or tried to kill their children? What was that disorder called?"

"Munchausen by proxy?" Karen questioned.

"That's it," Rob replied. He searched the Internet for information on Munchausen by proxy to refresh his memory of the disorder.

Munchausen syndrome by proxy, a very difficult disease to diagnose, is a form of child abuse, almost always by a mother, where unneeded medical attention is sought for a child. A mother will fake the child's symptoms or greatly exaggerate or even cause them by adding foreign and potentially lethal material into the child's food or bloodstream. The mother will doctor shop, taking the child from one doctor, clinic, and hospital to another, alleging a variety of real and imagined maladies. Some of the more common medical complaints are difficulty in breathing, asthma, blurry vision, and ear and sinus infections. The mother may fake symptoms by falsifying fevers or giving cathartics to induce vomiting or diarrhea. She may also infect IV lines to make the child appear or become ill. She is commonly seen as a devoted and unusually self-sacrificing mom, which can make medical providers unlikely to suspect the disease. It is generally considered an attention-seeking behavior, but it can be life-threatening to the child. It can and often does, in fact, result in the death of the child.

What seemed to jump out at Hall was that Gail White's description of Erin's disease matched many of the common areas that are associated with Munchausen by proxy. But more alarming to him was the IV or PICC line Erin had. Could Gail White have injected Erin with harmful substances through her PICC line? [4]

"I think I will have the police department run this by child protective services to see if it raises any red flags," he told his wife. The next day in his office, Hall retrieved the earlier newspaper article and reread it. While it slightly raised his eyebrows the first time, at second glance it really seemed suspect. He thought, what normal mother with a deathly sick child would thank her friends for kidnapping her and going out for drinks? What normal mother would describe her 10-year-old as "sicker than a dog" or make reference that "she is not a statistic and not in any book?" It just did not seem right.

He also did not understand why the Whites were claiming high medical expenses. The city had the Cadillac of health insurance plans that covered Mark White and his family with small, if any, co-pays or deductibles. Hall had never received any complaints from any employees or retirees over lack of healthcare coverage. And he had had employees who went through organ transplants, quadruple bypass surgery, the birth of premature babies, advanced stages of cancer, and others, none of whom experienced high out-of-pocket medical expenses. So why were the Whites having fund-raisers? It just did not seem to make sense to him.

The city manager called the head of the city's detective bureau, Captain Bill Owens, to his office. After reviewing the articles and discussing the medical issues, Captain Owens concurred that the entire situation was suspect. They agreed that it would be best to have experts at the county level investigate the situation to determine if there was some form of child abuse going on.

Experts at the county agreed, and an investigation was launched. But as is common, the wheels of justice seemed to turn slowly. The entire details of the investigation are beyond the scope of this book, but an example of the fraud and deceit by Gail White at the expense of her daughter should suffice.

Gail approached a friend and asked to borrow $3,000. She told the friend that she needed the money to pay off an outstanding balance at her daughter's allergy clinic. She said that the clinic had refused to see her daughter until this balance was paid. The friend agreed to loan her the $3,000 and wrote her a check from a home equity

---

[4] A televised documentary on Munchausen by proxy showed a secretly taped mother pouring chlorine bleach into her young daughter's IV feed.

line of credit. Upon learning this, City Manager Hall was even more troubled. His own son had gone to this same allergy clinic for an extended period of time, and all of the costs were covered by the city's health insurance.

Two days later Gail called her friend and said that her bank refused to cash or accept the check and asked if she could get it in cash. The friend agreed and gave her $3,000 in cash with Gail's assurance that she would tear up the check. The following month when the friend was reviewing her bank statement, she discovered that Gail had cashed her check on the same day that she gave it to her. The friend refused to press charges.

During the course of the investigation, Mark White applied for family medical leave. He was late for work one day, and in a possible attempt to avoid being disciplined, left the half-completed forms on the plant superintendent's desk, abruptly notified the supervisor that he was on family medical leave, and stormed out of the wastewater treatment plant. On his application, White stated as the reason for the leave "To be with my daughter at St. Jude Children's Research Hospital," and he listed a Dr. Melvin Cole as the treating physician.

The crescendo of the investigation stemmed from events at Elmberg's annual soccer association banquet held on September 17. Gail White attended the banquet unannounced and asked to address the crowd. The Association agreed to let her do so.

In a tearful address, Gail told the soccer players and their families to hug each other tight, especially parents, for "you may not have your child with you next year." She told them that Erin who had just turned 11 was not expected to see her twelfth birthday and begged for help with their mounting medical bills. As an example, she noted that Erin needed a walker and the insurance would not cover the cost.[5] Nearly sobbing, she told the soccer players and their families that they had incurred in excess of $27,000 in medical expenses and "it [the tally] continues to grow." She begged for help in her valiant, but probably futile, efforts to save Erin's life. When Gail was done, there was hardly a dry eye in the house. A hat was passed and over $800 was collected to help the White family. Even the two little boys who won the fifty/fifty raffle turned their winnings over to Gail to the thunderous applause of the crowd.

Upon hearing this the next day, City Manager Hall immediately contacted the city's healthcare provider. It was quickly determined that there was not $27,000 in outstanding medical claims. A few thousand dollars in claims were still being processed, but no claim had been denied. Hall had also thought it would be worth checking the tax-exempt status of the Erin Anne White Foundation. A check of both federal and state web sites showed no such foundation was listed as a legitimate charitable organization. It fact, its existence was nowhere to be found. When told this, Captain Owens showed the manager a copy of the flyer saying, "well it must be legitimate, they have a tax ID number." Hall explained that having a tax ID number

---

[5] The walker that Erin was using belonged to her grandmother. Even if the Whites had to buy a walker, its cost was minimal.

does not make one a charitable organization. Anyone or any organization can obtain a tax ID number. Every employer, public and private, is issued a tax ID number by the Internal Revenue Service.[6]

A few days later, Captain Owens approached the city manager, this time accompanied by the police chief, and asked if there was any proof that the Whites had even taken Erin to St. Jude Children's Hospital. Owens thought that maybe this whole episode was an attention-seeking hoax on their part. Hall explained that Mark White did, indeed, apply for family medical leave about 3 weeks earlier. On his application, he listed the dates his daughter would be at St. Jude and listed the treating physician and his telephone number. White also signed a full medical release form authorizing the City of Elmberg to review any and all medical records related to the requested leave. Hall, who also served as the city's personnel director, said he would try to verify the claim later in the day.

That afternoon, Hall placed the long-distance call to Dr. Melvin Cole at St. Jude Children's Research Hospital. When his receptionist answered the telephone, Hall explained that he simply needed to verify the dates a patient was at the hospital to see if they reconciled with those dates an employee, Mark White, had entered on his application. He said that he would fax them the signed medical release. The receptionist indicated that would be fine, and Hall expected she would return his call once she received the release. The receptionist asked, "What is the patient's name?"

"Erin White," Hall replied.

There was pause on the line, which lasted for a few seconds. The receptionist then blurted out, "I'll have Dr. Cole call you."

This took Hall back a bit. He found this very strange . . . very unusual. While he had not done this kind of thing often, he had done it a few times in his career. He had never had a doctor call him to verify appointment dates. His suspicions of Mrs. White mounted.

The following day, Dr. Cole returned the city manager's telephone call. When Hall answered, he explained to the doctor that he did not really expect to speak directly with him as he was just trying to verify appointment dates. Hall told him that the city was very concerned for the welfare of this child and Dr. Cole shared this concern. Hall asked if Dr. Cole could speak candidly about Erin's condition. Dr. Cole agreed. He told Hall that Erin was apparently a very sick girl, but he did not know why or know the source of her illness. He had yet to make a clear diagnosis.

Hall told Dr. Cole that the mother was quoted in the local paper saying that Erin had Warner's disease. Cole said that initially he thought it could be Warner's disease, but it was unlikely. He said every test for this disease came back negative, and he concluded Erin was not suffering from it and so advised the parents. Hall read almost

---

[6] It came to light in the course of litigation that the Whites' attorney for the foundation had applied to the Internal Revenue Service for tax-exempt status, and the application was denied. The Whites knew this, yet made the claim to potential donors.

all of the quotes Gail had made to the newspaper to Dr. Cole. His response to each was amazement. When told of the mother's comments that the doctors said Erin would probably not see her twelfth birthday, he seemed shocked and said, "No one here told her that!"

Dr. Cole told the city manager that Erin presented some medical conditions for which there were no logical explanations. For example, he said that Erin seemed unable to walk, yet there was no medical or physical reason for her not walking. He said that she could walk, but the mother had her convinced that she couldn't. When told of Gail's complaint that the insurance would not cover the cost of a walker, he nearly shouted, "That little girl does not need a walker!"

Dr. Cole asked Hall, "How well do you know Mrs. White?" Hall responded that he knew Mark White, as he was an employee of the city, but he had never met his wife. "She is a very unusual person," Dr. Cole elaborated. "She is very upset with me and the hospital. She wanted us to immediately begin cyclophosphamide or chemotherapy treatment on Erin. We would not start such an aggressive treatment unless a diagnosis supported it, and we have no diagnosis. She got very angry with us, and I mean *very* angry, when we refused to do so."

Hall told the doctor that the city's police department had begun a criminal investigation into the matter on suspicions of child abuse. He asked the doctor if he thought that this might be a case of Munchausen syndrome by proxy.

"It is interesting that you mention that," Dr. Cole said, "as we were just discussing that possibility this morning. The information that you have given me regarding the mother will be helpful in evaluating Erin's condition."

The telephone conversation ended with Hall asking the doctor if the city should be concerned that Erin's welfare could be in jeopardy each and every day that she was in the care of her mother. He responded, "Yes, I think that you should be." Not only was the city manager overly amazed at what Dr. Cole had told him, he was equally amazed that Dr. Cole *had* told him.

Hall discussed the conversation with the police chief and the detective captain, and it was agreed that some urgent action was required to remove Erin from the care of her mother. The next day, the detective bureau set up a sting operation. An undercover officer would call Gail White and tell her that he represented a generous benefactor who wanted to make a sizeable contribution to help defray Erin's medical bills that Gail discussed in her address at the soccer banquet. As there were no outstanding medical bills, if the Whites accepted this money, they would be committing an act of larceny by false pretenses, which would justify their immediate arrest.

The undercover officer contacted the Whites, and arrangements were made to meet at a local McDonald's restaurant. The officer wore a wire. The three sat for coffee, and Gail did most of the talking. She told the officer about her daughter's incurable disease, the frequent visits to St. Jude Hospital, and the mounting medical bills. During the relatively short visit, Gail was giddy . . . giggling and laughing . . . making jokes. Not the expected behavior of a mother whose 11-year-old daughter was on her deathbed. The undercover officer handed Mark $750 and he gladly accepted it. The three of them exited the restaurant, and the Whites profusely thanked the "benefactor." When they were in the middle of the parking lot, two previously hidden marked police cars pulled into the lot and arrested the pair.

The department youth officer, along with two representatives from Child Protective Services, went to the Whites' home and collected the three children, who were quickly placed in the temporary custody of their grandparents. Also at the station, it was discovered that there was an outstanding warrant for Gail's arrest on a shoplifting charge.[7] Mark was released that evening, but Gail was held overnight on the outstanding warrant.

As expected, news of the arrests garnered a bit of media attention, and it was broadcast on area radio and television stations. After one of the evening broadcasts aired, the telephone rang at City Manager Hall's home. It was his eldest daughter. Without even saying hello, she screamed at her father, "Dad, how could you let your police arrest Gail White! She has a very ill young daughter who is dying! How could you let this happen and take that poor little girl away from her mother?" Hall tried to calm his daughter down, but she continued to rant and rave. "Gail told us just yesterday at the beauty salon that she was bringing Erin in on Saturday to have her head shaved and fitted for a wig because she was going to lose all her hair when the chemotherapy began next week!"

While it seemed like nothing could surprise Hall anymore when it came to Gail White, even this was a bit over the edge. He assured his daughter that there was more to the eye of what she was seeing and he would fill her in more on the facts later.

The following morning, Captain Owens came to the manager's office and handed him a slip of paper. In Gail's writing the note named another St. Jude doctor and his phone number. Owens reported, "She handed this note to me this morning and said that this doctor is faxing over to Erin's allergist a letter confirming that Erin has Warner's disease." "Okay," replied Hall, "I'll call him." And, indeed he did.

The name Gail had given was Dr. Glenn Bishop. Hall called Dr. Bishop's office and when he mentioned the patient's name as Erin White, he got a similar abrupt, "I'll have the doctor call you," as when he called Dr. Cole's office. Later that day, Dr. Bishop called the city manager. Hall advised Dr. Bishop of Gail White's arrest on suspicion of child abuse and that she told the police that he was faxing a letter to Erin's allergist confirming the diagnosis of Warner's disease. "Nothing could be further from the truth," Dr. Bishop advised. "No such letter is being faxed." Hall reviewed the news articles with Dr. Bishop, and Bishop had the same reaction of shock and surprise at what Gail was saying as Dr. Cole had. He was particularly troubled by the latest revelation of her plans to have the little girl's head shaved. He felt that Mrs. White's actions and comments were very bizarre.

Gail White posted bond and was released from the city's lockup. She was given several court dates, as was her husband Mark, and they were forbidden from having

[7] This was the second time in an 18-month period that Gail had been caught shoplifting.

any unsupervised contact with their children. For the next 2 months, the children remained in the care and custody of their grandparents. Within the first few weeks, Erin's health began to improve dramatically. The walker was soon gone and she could walk unassisted. The PICC line was removed, she returned to school, and she began participating in gym and other physical activities.

Over the next 2 months, the family went through a battery of interviews, tests, examinations, and observations. This was done by psychiatrists, psychologists, social workers, child specialists, and others. As to the Munchausen by proxy diagnosis, it was a split decision. Some thought it was; some thought it wasn't. All but one concluded that Erin suffered from child abuse at the hands of her mother and, to a lesser extent, her father by acquiescence.

After this 2-month period, the children were returned to the Whites, subject to supposedly indefinite strict monitoring by Child Protective Services. The authorities opted not to prosecute Mark and Gail White on any of the charges. But the city's objective to prevent further harm to their daughter Erin was achieved. As of this writing, Erin is a healthy 13-year-old junior high school student and an active participant in a variety of sports. Her allergist believes she no longer suffers from asthma.

In a most ironic twist to this saga, years after the Whites' arrest, the city subpoenaed Erin's medical records as part of its defense in a lawsuit filed by the Whites against the city and its manager and police officers.[8] In the doctor's notes from when Erin was 9, a year before the news articles were published, the following entry was uncovered: "May be Munchausen by proxy due to all the doctor shopping." The child's own doctor had suspected this very early on.

Questions

1. Was City Manager Hall acting beyond the scope of his authority in suspecting Munchausen by proxy when he had no medical training?[9]

2. Was it unethical of the city manager to discuss the medical condition of Erin with her doctors? Was it unethical of them to discuss it with him?

3. Was it unethical for family and friends of the Whites to hold a fund-raiser and distribute canisters for donations? Should they have checked out Gail's story first?

4. Was it inappropriate for the city manager to connect his leisure activity of reading true crime books to his responsibilities with the city?

---

[8] After reviewing an extensive record relating to the Whites' claims, a superior court judge dismissed the lawsuit, stating that the city's officials' and police officers' actions in this matter were perfectly reasonable in protecting the welfare of this child.

[9] This argument was aggressively pursued by the Whites' attorneys in their lawsuit against him and the city.

5. Was it appropriate for the manager to be suspicious of the newspaper articles just because no doctors were quoted?

6. Were the city manager's actions justified just because he did not like Gail White's quotes in the newspaper?

7. Could not the high medical costs mentioned by Gail White have been for travel, lodging, and other costs associated with Erin's illness not covered by insurance? Should not Hall have considered this possibility?

8. Was the city manager overly involved in what was essentially a criminal investigation? If so, why? If not, what would justify his actions?

9. Both Hall's wife and daughter believed Gail White. Was it unethical of him to discuss the case with his wife? With his daughter?

10. Did the police overreact when they arrested the Whites based mostly on Hall's telephone conversation with Dr. Cole? Was their lying to the Whites about the generous benefactor unethical? If it was, could this unethical behavior on their part be justified? If so, on what grounds?

11. What do you think would have happened if the city had not interceded in this matter or if the city manager did not direct the police department to look into it?

Chapter 21

Hire the Hard-Core Unemployed

"The time has come to reverse the flow of power and resources from the states and communities to Washington, and start power and resources flowing back from Washington to the states and communities and more important, to the people, all across America . . ."

—President Richard M. Nixon, 1971

We began this book with a case study involving C.E.T.A. employment. So, too, we will end with case studies on these special gifts from the federal government to local governments.

In 1972, Congress passed and President Richard Nixon signed the State and Local Fiscal Assistance Act. It was quickly dubbed *federal revenue sharing.*

In announcing the federal revenue sharing program, states and local governments geared up for a windfall of billions of dollars in federal aid. For the most part, expenditure of these funds was unrestricted. State and local governments could spend the money in almost any fashion they chose. These funds were distributed with little regard to need. Both the poorest and wealthiest communities nationally received funds on a formula based mostly on population.

The more astute and intelligent communities spent their funds on nonrecurring projects, recognizing that these funds might not last forever. They built city halls, police stations, fire stations, and libraries. They improved their roads, water mains, sewer mains, and other infrastructure capital with these federal funds. The less astute and not-so-intelligent government officials used their federal revenue sharing funds for operations. They hired more police officers or firefighters, hired assistants, or found other ways to increase local public employment. They did not give thought to what would happen when these funds dried up, which they surely would, and did.

Faced with a mounting federal deficit in the mid- to late-1980s, President Ronald Reagan convinced Congress to end federal revenue sharing in 1987. He told local communities in the country that the federal government no longer had revenue to share. Those cities that had used these federal funds for capital projects did not feel the pinch as hard as those that had used the money for operations. These latter ones either absorbed the cost with local funds or laid off employees.

The 1970s also saw a monetary windfall to local governments in the form of various categorical grant programs to address nationally defined priorities. Most notably, billions of dollars were given to local governments for wastewater treatment plants to provide secondary and even tertiary treatment for sewage water prior to discharge into our nation's lakes and streams. That program resulted in environmental benefits that are still enjoyed to this day. Those plants built with federal dollars in the 70s and 80s continue to serve thousands of communities.

During these freewheeling 70s, the Nixon administration launched another massive grant program for local governments. The impact of the program is still being felt, though waning, to this day. Unfortunately, in many cases that impact was not as positive a one as the wastewater treatment program was. In this book, other case studies have mentioned the Comprehensive Employment and Training Act of 1973, more commonly referred to by its acronym C.E.T.A. Those studies make allusions to some of this act's shortcomings. Here we take a little closer look at C.E.T.A. and examine three individual participants.

President Nixon felt that the country needed a federal program to provide job-training skills to the long-term unemployed. He felt that at nearly 6%, the nation's unemployment rate was too high, and he modeled C.E.T.A. after the successful Works Progress Administration (W.P.A.) during the Great Depression. Under the W.P.A., the Roosevelt administration directly hired the unemployed and placed them on federal public works projects. The unemployment rate in 1972 was nowhere near the peak 24.9% it was in 1932, so as to justify such a broad sweeping jobs program like C.E.T.A. If its success was to be measured by a reduction in the unemployment rate, it was a dismal failure. During C.E.T.A.'s 9-year run, the nation's unemployment rate peaked at 8.5% in 1975 and at best returned to 1972 levels in 1979. The unemployment rate then began to climb again and peaked at just under 10% in 1982 when C.E.T.A. was replaced by the Job Training Partnership Act, which was not an employment program.

The basic premise of C.E.T.A. was to provide money to local governments to hire and train workers to develop marketable skills, which would allow them to move to an unsubsidized job. Unfortunately, this basic premise was fundamentally flawed.

For the most part, it just did not work that way. The theory was "Let's give local government lots and lots of money to hire the hard-core unemployed—people who cannot find a job anywhere else. No one will hire them; they have no skills; they have no training. But let's give local government the money to hire them and *make them police officers and firefighters!*"[1] Here we examine three cases that went awry.

Real Estate Agent Turned Police Officer

Lonnie Knight was an unemployed real estate agent. His dream to become wealthy in the real estate market was quickly fading. Real estate sales in Melville had plummeted due to record high interest rates and a poor economy. The unemployment rate had also skyrocketed and Knight had become one of its latest victims. He had been out of work for well over a year but kept up his membership and activities with the local Lions club. This was his good fortune as another long-term Lions club member was Melville's city manager, who was nearing retirement after 22 years with the city. The city manager made Knight aware of the C.E.T.A. program and asked the 38-year-old out-of-work real estate agent if he would be interested in changing careers to law enforcement. Knight said that he had not really thought much about such a change, but, after all, he did need a job. Off he went to the police academy and joined Melville's police department 8 weeks later.

His first year or two on the force were mostly uneventful, although the city received a complaint or two over his mannerisms and attitude. By his third year, however, the complaints escalated. His short temper and foul mouth would result in discipline for almost any other officer. However, being a buddy of the city manager essentially made him untouchable, and no disciplinary record was ever made. The police chief supposedly counseled him on occasion but nothing was ever put in writing. At the end of Officer Knight's third year with the force, the city manager retired and in came a new city manager. Jon Vogle arrived and took the reins of Melville in January.

While young and relatively new to city management, Vogle did bring with him 3 years of experience in another, smaller community. The problems with Officer Knight quickly surfaced to the manager's attention. In his first 6 months, Vogle received as many complaints regarding Knight's job performance. The most common complaints were over his loud verbal outbursts and his hot temper. Knight had a short fuse—a very short fuse. Vogle directed the police chief to document these incidents and to begin progressive discipline. Over the next several months, Knight received three written reprimands and two verbal ones. He filed a grievance each time and each one required a hearing before City Manager Vogle. At each of these hearings, Knight was his own worst enemy. He was tense and his face was beet red

---

[1] In fairness, not all communities used C.E.T.A. funds only for police and fire positions. Maintenance workers, park attendants, and the like were also hired.

at each hearing. He looked as if he was going to explode. Vogle quickly ascertained this man had no business owning a gun, let alone carrying one as part of his official job duties. The manager wanted Knight's errant behavior documented to build a case for termination. He felt that Knight had neither the skills nor the temperament to be in law enforcement.

In late summer, Knight was on routine patrol late in the evening in Melville when he spotted his estranged wife (who had moved to another part of the state) at a gas station. He approached her in his patrol car and began yelling at her with a long string of profanities over their marital discord. He threatened to beat the living daylights out of her. She rebuffed his attack and quickly drove off. Dissatisfied that he had not completed his discussions with her, he took off in pursuit. As his wife was in fear for her safety, she raced out of town with Knight, in the city patrol car, hot on her tail.

For nearly an hour and a half, he chased her over miles of back roads. Eventually, county sheriff units were in pursuit of him. The chase came to an end when he finally ran his estranged wife's car off the road and into a ditch. The sheriff's unit arrived at the same time and the sheriff had to restrain him from attacking his wife. Knight returned to the city and finished his shift.

When the police chief informed City Manager Vogle of the incident the next morning, he directed that Knight be terminated. In a plea deal with the police officers' union, Knight was given a last chance reprieve. Under this deal, he would be given a 30-day nonpaid suspension and would only be cleared to return to work when a licensed psychiatrist stated in writing that he was fit for duty as a police officer. The deal also made it very clear that if he returned to work, any future infractions, even minor ones, would result in his immediate termination with no right of appeal.

While on his suspension, Knight was examined by a psychiatrist mutually agreed to by the city and the union. The psychiatrist administered routine personality and other tests to Knight. Three weeks later, he submitted his findings to City Manager Vogle. In his report, the doctor stated that Knight passed all tests, was not delusional, and did not have any personality disorders. The psychiatrist not only determined that Knight was fit for duty, he added that it was important that he return to work as soon as possible as he greatly missed his lifelong desire to be in law enforcement. This lifelong desire, of course, began at age 38 courtesy of the C.E.T.A. program.

The Monday before Thanksgiving was a normal day in Melville; relatively quiet. The evening council meeting was also uneventful, though it lasted a bit longer than usual. As he exited the city council chambers, City Manager Vogle was met by the police chief. The inevitable had happened. Once again, Knight lost his cool. He had arrested a juvenile who was wanted for vandalism. At the police station, the dispatcher called in other officers on the street to pull Knight away from the youngster. He was screaming and swearing at the kid and had kicked him several times in his uncontrollable rage. It was then learned that Knight had forged the warrant for the juvenile's arrest.

"That's it," exclaimed Vogle. "Fire him!" Knight was summarily discharged that evening.

Five days later, on the Saturday after Thanksgiving, City Manager Vogle was home. It was an unseasonably warm afternoon, and he was raking leaves. His wife called out to him, telling him that he had a telephone call and that it sounded urgent. He rushed into his home and picked up the receiver. On the other end of the line was the police chief, informing him that Knight's body was just discovered in the basement of his home. Knight had jerry-rigged a shotgun, placed the barrel in his mouth, and blew his head off. Knight was 43.

Not in the Line of Duty

Donald Morgan was a 25-year-old unemployed laborer. He had been out of work for nearly 2 years, living on public assistance. To his credit, he did earn his GED during this hiatus. He had applied for numerous jobs, but his lack of formal education and limited skills hindered his job-seeking efforts. His luck changed when he was hired by the Cyprus Grove police department in the late 70s. He was urged to apply by his next-door neighbor, a retired police officer. The retiree had heard of the department's new police cadet program funded with federal C.E.T.A. funds. The retiree thought Morgan would easily meet the program's requirements.

Morgan served as a cadet for 2 years, and then the city absorbed his cost and made him a member of the regular force. Over the next 20 years, he served the department not with great distinction but not with any serious disciplinary problems, either. With the exception of a 2-year stint with a countywide drug enforcement task force, he served in the road patrol unit of the department. Even though department brass did not feel that Morgan was good supervisory material, that did not prevent him from being promoted. He always tested well in the city's antiquated Civil Service system, and the city was left with little choice but to promote him. And promote him it did. First to corporal, then to sergeant, and finally to lieutenant in charge of the midnight shift. He held this position for the last of his 2 years with Cyprus Grove's police department, prior to his abrupt departure.

One warm August evening, two detectives were working undercover conducting surveillance in an area of Cyprus Grove known for drug trafficking. Their efforts were rewarded when they observed four young people, two males and two females, exchange money and drugs under a dimming corner streetlight. After the detectives called for backup, the four were arrested and charged with misdemeanor offenses. Back at Cyprus Grove's police headquarters, the foursome were separated by gender and interviewed. The two females thought they might have a chance to get out of the situation if they offered the detectives some damaging information about one of their own. The girls were known better by their stage names, Destiny and Chastity. They were exotic dancers at a local gentlemen's club. They also told detectives that they made their real money as prostitutes. The two 24-year-olds had each been in this self-employed business for 2 years and one of their best customers was none other than the midnight shift supervisor, Lieutenant Don Morgan.

Not only was Morgan a regular customer, but he purchased their services while on duty. Sometimes he would go to their apartment and sometimes he would take them to his own home in a neighboring community. They said that if time were short they would engage in sex acts in his marked police car. They told the detectives that this happened on a near weekly basis and had been taking place for well over a year.

When confronted with their accusations, Morgan vehemently denied them. He accused them of making up the tale because they did not like it when he occasionally chased them off their favorite corner. He asked his supervisors why they would believe the lies of a couple of hookers over the truths of a 20-year veteran of the police department. He was not going to let his career be shortened by a couple of malcontented ladies of the evening.

However, there was an air of sincerity in the girls' story. They told the detectives that they were not upset with Morgan because he occasionally moved them off their corner. They were mad because he owed them money for services rendered. They eagerly agreed to be wired to prove that they were telling the truth.

Apparently, the revelation did not persuade Morgan to lay low for a while. While on routine patrol 3 days later, he saw Destiny and Chastity as they were leaving the club. He then was the subject of the detectives' surveillance. They had hidden a secret recording device in his patrol vehicle. They felt this would be more effective than directly wiring the girls. Morgan invited the girls to get into his scout car, and they did. He drove around Cyprus Grove, stopping from time to time in back alleys. The detectives observed what appeared to be suspicious behavior on the lieutenant's part and were anxious to listen to the recording device at the end of his shift.

After Lieutenant Morgan turned his scout car in, the detectives quickly reclaimed the recorder. It contained enough incriminating evidence to charge Morgan with soliciting and accosting a prostitute. The detectives met with the police chief, who, in turn, met with City Manager Tammi Burgess. The city manager was livid. "Here," she thought, "is a man being paid to uphold the law and he's breaking it; and he's breaking it while in uniform and on duty!" She told the chief to immediately terminate him and charge him with multiple misdemeanor charges for each and every time the girls could document time spent with him. The chief reminded her that there were certain procedures that had to be followed first both under Civil Service rules and the labor contract. There first had to be a chief's hearing at which Morgan would be allowed to explain and defend his actions. "Give the guilty perverted bastard his hearing, then fire him!" the manager shouted to the chief.

The detectives confronted Lieutenant Morgan with the solid evidence. After the detectives played the tape, the cornered lieutenant confessed. Before he said anything further, he asked to speak with his union representatives, and the detectives agreed. However, he was ordered to surrender his badge and police ID. The following day, the union business agent presented an offer to City Manager Burgess. He told her that Morgan would resign effective immediately, defer his retirement, and let the record show that he was demoted to sergeant. Burgess said no. She wanted him terminated and prosecuted to the fullest extent of the law. The union officials said that if that happened, they would fully defend him and appeal the termination to binding arbitration. After haggling back and forth, the parties reached an agreement.

Lieutenant Morgan agreed to resign immediately. He would be demoted to patrol officer so that payouts for unused time would be at the patrol officer's rate, and his retirement would be deferred until he reached age 55. He was not criminally prosecuted.

The Wandering Firefighter

Pete Coryell had been city manager of Lotis for nearly 20 years. Several years ago, prior to the current fire chief's appointment, Coryell had to assume the role of acting fire department manager. The fire chief at the time had retired and a replacement had not yet been named. On his first day of this temporary duty, he stopped by the fire station for some routine paperwork.

As he was about to leave, Fire Lieutenant Bob Carson stopped him in the hallway. "Mr. Coryell," he called out. "Can I talk to you about something?"

"Sure," Coryell responded. The lieutenant, with his arms flailing and voiced raised explained, "Mr. Coryell. Every fire station in the United States of America . . . *in the United States of America* . . . has three refrigerators . . . one for each shift!" He then led Coryell into the station's kitchen area and showed him the two refrigerators wedged between a wall and a countertop cabinet. With his hands shaped for a karate chop he showed Coryell, as if he were cutting the cabinet, he said, "Now see, here we can cut out this cabinet right here because we do not use this countertop to cut our meat on any more. We bought that cutting board over there," he said, pointing to one near the sink, "to cut our meat on now because we can wash it in really hot water, don't want to cut on this counter anymore, you know because of the salmonella thing. And we can just cut this counter out right here and the third refrigerator will slide right in!" He continued, with his arms still flailing, "Because God forbid, you come off a 4-day Kelly [2] and it's the peak of the tomato season, and I mean the peak of the tomato season, and," he gasped "you go to the refrigerator and there is no mayonnaise!" [3] Carson was dead serious. He was another of the city's hard-core unemployed hired under the C.E.T.A. program in 1976. His 30-plus-year career with the fire department only recently came to an abrupt end.

A 911 call came in to the city's dispatch, reporting smoke coming from the roof of a restaurant about eight blocks away from the city's fire station. Carson was alone in the fire department when the call came in as the other firefighters/EMTs were on an

---

[2] A 4-day Kelly is when a firefighter gets 3 days off in his or her rotation, and about every 2 months a 4th day is added on; this was supposedly invented by a New York firefighter by the name of Kelly.

[3] Only an astute city manager would note that in John Travolta's movie *Ladder 49*, the Baltimore fire station only has two refrigerators.

ambulance run. He asked the dispatcher, "Yeah, well what do you want me to do about it? I'm here by myself."

Just then, Fire Chief Nelson arrived from another part of the building and told Carson to respond with the fire engine and he would follow in the pickup truck. As they arrived on the scene, two fire trucks from a neighboring city were already en route under the communities' mutual aid pact. Carson put on his turnout gear and breathing tank, climbed the outdoor stairs on the building and began to attack the fire. He was soon assisted by the neighboring firefighters. Meanwhile, the fire chief donned the mandatory incident commander vest and directed the fire scene. Apparently agitated that the chief, who had only been with the department 14 years, had taken command of the scene, Carson threw down his air tank and exchanged words with the chief. All this time the structure was on fire. After angrily declaring, "I can't take this anymore!" Carson stormed off the scene. In full turnout gear and covered in soot, he harrumphed all the way back to the fire station, incredulously, leaving the scene of a working fire! Seeing him stomping down the sidewalk, an off-duty police officer stopped to see if he needed help. In a string of profanities, Carson said that he just couldn't take it anymore.

When Carson arrived at the fire station, he removed his turnout gear, checked himself out, and went home. The next day as Coryell was reading the chief's report of the fire lieutenant's leaving the scene of a working fire, the local firefighters' union president appeared in his doorway. He handed the city manager a memorandum from the union recommending that Carson receive a commendation for heroism for single-handedly fighting the fire before he left. After the union president left, Coryell just shook his head in disgust. He called the fire chief and directed him to immediately terminate Carson and directed the police to charge him with a misdemeanor criminal charge of willful neglect of duty.

The union, of course, filed a grievance and demanded the lieutenant's immediate reinstatement. The union officials felt he did nothing wrong, or at least that was the position their attorney verbalized. The city countered that it would rescind the termination under the following conditions:

- The lieutenant would be demoted to the rank of firefighter.
- All payouts for accumulated sick and vacation time would be at the firefighter rate.
- He would accept a 60-day unpaid, disciplinary suspension.
- He would submit a signed letter of resignation effective the last day of his suspension.
- Upon acceptance of the required letter of resignation, he would be allowed to begin his retirement.

This was not acceptable to the union. Its executive board met with the city manager and seemed to understand the seriousness of the lieutenant's negligence. The union officers just wanted the city to allow him to retire. The city manager agreed he would allow such if they simply would withdraw their grievance and let the termination of the lieutenant stand. They verbally agreed and then consulted with their attorney. Their attorney prepared a grievance settlement document that provided the following:

- The lieutenant would provide the city with a letter setting forth his voluntary termination.
- Any and all documents relating to his discharge would be expunged from his personnel file.
- Any requests for information were to indicate that his employment ended by way of a voluntary termination.
- His application for retirement would be processed and benefits initiated as soon as possible.

This was unacceptable to City Manager Coryell. He told the firefighters' union officers that the lieutenant crossed a line that a firefighter should never cross. "He left the scene of a working fire!" Coryell exclaimed. After considerable persuasion and over their union attorney's objection, the union officers withdrew the grievance and the termination was upheld.

Questions

1. Was City Manager Vogle partially responsible for Officer Knight's suicide?
2. Was it unethical for Vogle to terminate Knight so close to a holiday?
3. Should Vogle have sent Knight to an anger management program in an effort to retrain him?
4. Was there just cause to immediately terminate Lonnie Knight after he chased his estranged wife with the city's patrol vehicle?
5. Was it unethical for Burgess to assume Morgan's guilt without first holding a hearing to determine his defense of his actions?
6. Was it unethical for her to agree to dropping criminal charges against Morgan in light of his admission of guilt?
7. Was Coryell's firing of Carson too harsh a punishment especially in light of his 30 years with the city?
8. Were criminal charges against Carson justified?
9. What exactly is a voluntary termination? Would this be considered firing oneself?

Codes of Ethics

International City/County Management Association Code of Ethics[1]

The ICMA Code of Ethics was adopted by the ICMA membership in 1924, and most recently amended by the membership in May 1998. The Guidelines for the Code were adopted by the ICMA Executive Board in 1972, and most recently revised in July 2004.

The mission of ICMA is to create excellence in local governance by developing and fostering professional local government management worldwide. To further this mission, certain principles, as enforced by the Rules of Procedure, shall govern the conduct of every member of ICMA, who shall:

1. Be dedicated to the concepts of effective and democratic local government by responsible elected officials and believe that professional general management is essential to the achievement of this objective.

2. Affirm the dignity and worth of the services rendered by government and maintain a constructive, creative, and practical attitude toward local government affairs and a deep sense of social responsibility as a trusted public servant.

Guideline

Advice to Officials of Other Local Governments

When members advise and respond to inquiries from elected or appointed officials of other local governments, they should inform the administrators of those communities.

3. Be dedicated to the highest ideals of honor and integrity in all public and personal relationships in order that the member may merit the respect and confidence of the elected officials, of other officials and employees, and of the public.

Guidelines

Public Confidence

Members should conduct themselves so as to maintain public confidence in their profession, their local government, and in their performance of the public trust.

Impression of Influence

Members should conduct their official and personal affairs in such a manner as to give the clear impression that they cannot be improperly influenced in the performance of their official duties.

Appointment Commitment

Members who accept an appointment to a position should not fail to report for that position. This does not preclude the possibility of a member considering several offers or seeking several positions at the same time, but once a *bona fide* offer of a position has been accepted, that commitment should be honored. Oral acceptance of an employment offer is considered binding unless the employer makes fundamental changes in terms of employment.

Credentials

An application for employment or for ICMA's Voluntary Credentialing Program should be complete and accurate as to all pertinent details of education, experience, and personal history. Members should recognize that both omissions and inaccuracies must be avoided.

Professional Respect

Members seeking a management position should show professional respect for persons formerly holding the position or for others who might be applying for the same position. Professional respect does not preclude honest differences of opinion; it does preclude attacking a person's motives or integrity in order to be appointed to a position.

Reporting Ethics Violations

When becoming aware of a possible violation of the ICMA Code of Ethics, members are encouraged to report the matter to ICMA. In reporting the matter, members may choose to go on record as the complainant or report the matter on a confidential basis.

Confidentiality

Members should not discuss or divulge information with anyone about pending or completed ethics cases, except as specifically authorized by the Rules of Procedure for Enforcement of the Code of Ethics.

Seeking Employment

Members should not seek employment for a position having an incumbent administrator who has not resigned or been officially informed that his or her services are to be terminated.

    4. Recognize that the chief function of local government at all times is to serve the best interests of all of the people.

Guideline

Length of Service

A minimum of two years generally is considered necessary in order to render a professional service to the local government. A short tenure should be the exception rather than a recurring experience. However, under special circumstances, it may be in the best interests of the local government and the member to separate in a shorter time. Examples of such circumstances would include refusal of the appointing authority to honor commitments concerning conditions of employment, a vote of no confidence in the member, or severe personal problems. It is the responsibility of an applicant for a position to ascertain conditions of employment. Inadequately determining terms of employment prior to arrival does not justify premature termination.

    5. Submit policy proposals to elected officials; provide them with facts and advice on matters of policy as a basis for making decisions and setting community goals; and uphold and implement local government policies adopted by elected officials.

Guideline

Conflicting Roles

Members who serve multiple roles—working as both city attorney and city manager for the same community, for example—should avoid participating in matters that create the appearance of a conflict of interest. They should disclose the potential conflict to the governing body so that other opinions may be solicited.

6. Recognize that elected representatives of the people are entitled to the credit for the establishment of local government policies; responsibility for policy execution rests with the members.

7. Refrain from all political activities which undermine public confidence in professional administrators. Refrain from participation in the election of the members of the employing legislative body.

Guidelines

Elections of the Governing Body

Members should maintain a reputation for serving equally and impartially all members of the governing body of the local government they serve, regardless of party. To this end, they should not engage in active participation in the election campaign on behalf of or in opposition to candidates for the governing body.

Elections of Elected Executives

Members should not engage in the election campaign of any candidate for mayor or elected county executive.

Running for Office

Members shall not run for elected office or become involved in political activities related to running for elected office. They shall not seek political endorsements, financial contributions or engage in other campaign activities.

Elections

Members share with their fellow citizens the right and responsibility to vote and to voice their opinion on public issues. However, in order not to impair their effectiveness on behalf of the local governments they serve, they shall not participate in political activities to support the candidacy of individuals running for any city, county, special district, school, state or federal offices. Specifically, they shall not endorse candidates, make financial contributions, sign or circulate petitions, or participate in fund-raising activities for individuals seeking or holding elected office.

Elections on the Council-Manager Plan

Members may assist in preparing and presenting materials that explain the council-manager form of government to the public prior to an election on the use of the plan. If assistance is required by another community, members may respond. All activities regarding ballot issues should be conducted within local regulations and in a professional manner.

Presentation of Issues

Members may assist the governing body in presenting issues involved in referenda such as bond issues, annexations, and similar matters.

8. Make it a duty continually to improve the member's professional ability and to develop the competence of associates in the use of management techniques.

Guidelines

Self-Assessment

Each member should assess his or her professional skills and abilities on a periodic basis.

Professional Development

Each member should commit at least 40 hours per year to professional development activities that are based on the practices identified by the members of ICMA.

9. Keep the community informed on local government affairs; encourage communication between the citizens and all local government officers; emphasize friendly and courteous service to the public; and seek to improve the quality and image of public service.

10. Resist any encroachment on professional responsibilities, believing the member should be free to carry out official policies without interference, and handle each problem without discrimination on the basis of principle and justice.

Guideline

Information Sharing

The member should openly share information with the governing body while diligently carrying out the member's responsibilities as set forth in the charter or enabling legislation.

11. Handle all matters of personnel on the basis of merit so that fairness and impartiality govern a member's decisions pertaining to appointments, pay adjustments, promotions, and discipline.

Guideline

Equal Opportunity

All decisions pertaining to appointments, pay adjustments, promotions, and discipline should prohibit discrimination because of race, color, religion, sex, national origin, sexual orientation, political affiliation, disability, age, or marital status.

It should be the members' personal and professional responsibility to actively recruit and hire a diverse staff throughout their organizations.

12. Seek no favor; believe that personal aggrandizement or profit secured by confidential information or by misuse of public time is dishonest.

Guidelines

Gifts

Members should not directly or indirectly solicit any gift or accept or receive any gift—whether it be money, services, loan, travel, entertainment, hospitality, promise, or any other form—under the following circumstances: (1) it could be reasonably inferred or expected that the gift was intended to influence them in the performance of their official duties; or (2) the gift was intended to serve as a reward for any official action on their part.

It is important that the prohibition of unsolicited gifts be limited to circumstances related to improper influence. In *de minimus* situations, such as meal checks, some modest maximum dollar value should be determined by the member as a guideline. The guideline is not intended to isolate members from normal social practices where gifts among friends, associates, and relatives are appropriate for certain occasions.

Investments in Conflict with Official Duties

Member[s] should not invest or hold any investment, directly or indirectly, in any financial business, commercial, or other private transaction that creates a conflict with their official duties.

In the case of real estate, the potential use of confidential information and knowledge to further a member's personal interest requires special consideration. This guideline recognizes that members' official actions and decisions can be influenced if there is a conflict with personal investments. Purchases and sales which might be interpreted as speculation for quick profit ought to be avoided (see the guideline on "Confidential Information").

Because personal investments may prejudice or may appear to influence official actions and decisions, members may, in concert with their governing body, provide for disclosure of such investments prior to accepting their position as local government administrator or prior to any official action by the governing body that may affect such investments.

Personal Relationships

Members should disclose any personal relationship to the governing body in any instance where there could be the appearance of a conflict of interest. For example, if the manager's spouse works for a developer doing business with the local government, that fact should be disclosed.

Confidential Information

Members should not disclose to others, or use to further their personal interest, confidential information acquired by them in the course of their official duties.

Private Employment

Members should not engage in, solicit, negotiate for, or promise to accept private employment, nor should they render services for private interests or conduct a private business when such employment, service, or business creates a conflict with or impairs the proper discharge of their official duties.

Teaching, lecturing, writing, or consulting are typical activities that may not involve conflict of interest, or impair the proper discharge of their official duties. Prior notification of the appointing authority is appropriate in all cases of outside employment.

Representation

Members should not represent any outside interest before any agency, whether public or private, except with the authorization of or at the direction of the appointing authority they serve.

Endorsements

Members should not endorse commercial products or services by agreeing to use their photograph, endorsement, or quotation in paid or other commercial advertisements, whether or not for compensation. Members may, however, agree to endorse the following, provided they do not receive any compensation: (1) books or other publications; (2) professional development or educational services provided by non-profit membership organizations or recognized educational institutions; (3) products and/or services in which the local government has a direct economic interest.

Members' observations, opinions, and analyses of commercial products used or tested by their local governments are appropriate and useful to the profession when included as part of professional articles and reports.

American Society for Public Administration Code of Ethics (1994 Version)[2]

In 1981 the American Society for Public Administration's National Council adopted a set of moral principles. Three years later in 1984, the Council approved a Code of Ethics for ASPA members. In 1994 that Code was superseded by this one.

The American Society for Public Administration (ASPA) exists to advance the science, processes, and art of public administration. The Society affirms its responsibility to develop the spirit of professionalism within its membership, and to increase public awareness of ethical principles in public service by its example. To this end, we, the members of the Society, commit ourselves to the following principles:

I. Serve the Public Interest

Serve the public, beyond serving oneself. ASPA members are committed to:

1. Exercise discretionary authority to promote the public interest.
2. Oppose all forms of discrimination and harassment, and promote affirmative action.
3. Recognize and support the public's right to know the public's business.
4. Involve citizens in policy decision-making.
5. Exercise compassion, benevolence, fairness and optimism.
6. Respond to the public in ways that are complete, clear, and easy to understand.
7. Assist citizens in their dealings with government.
8. Be prepared to make decisions that may not be popular.

[2]Courtesy of the American Society for Public Administration.

II. Respect the Constitution and the Law

Respect, support, and study government constitutions and laws that define responsibilities of public agencies, employees, and all citizens. ASPA members are committed to:

1. Understand and apply legislation and regulations relevant to their professional role.
2. Work to improve and change laws and policies that are counterproductive or obsolete.
3. Eliminate unlawful discrimination.
4. Prevent all forms of mismanagement of public funds by establishing and maintaining strong fiscal and management controls, and by supporting audits and investigative activities.
5. Respect and protect privileged information.
6. Encourage and facilitate legitimate dissent activities in government and protect the whistle blowing rights of public employees.
7. Promote constitutional principles of equality, fairness, representativeness, responsiveness and due process in protecting citizens' rights.

III. Demonstrate Personal Integrity

Demonstrate the highest standards in all activities to inspire public confidence and trust in public service. ASPA members are committed to:

1. Maintain truthfulness and honesty and to not compromise them for advancement, honor, or personal gain.
2. Ensure that others receive credit for their work and contributions.
3. Zealously guard against conflict of interest or its appearance: e.g., nepotism, improper outside employment, misuse of public resources or the acceptance of gifts.
4. Respect superiors, subordinates, colleagues and the public.
5. Take responsibility for their errors.
6. Conduct official acts without partisanship.

IV. Promote Ethical Organizations

Strengthen organizational capabilities to apply ethics, efficiency and effectiveness in serving the public. ASPA members are committed to:

1. Enhance organizational capacity for open communication, creativity, and dedication.
2. Subordinate institutional loyalties to the public good.

3. Establish procedures that promote ethical behavior and hold individuals and organizations accountable for their conduct.

4. Provide organization members with an administrative means for dissent, assurance of due process and safeguards against reprisal.

5. Promote merit principles that protect against arbitrary and capricious actions.

6. Promote organizational accountability through appropriate controls and procedures.

7. Encourage organizations to adopt, distribute, and periodically review a code of ethics as a living document.

V. Strive for Professional Excellence

Strengthen individual capabilities and encourage the professional development of others. ASPA members are committed to:

1. Provide support and encouragement to upgrade competence.

2. Accept as a personal duty the responsibility to keep up to date on emerging issues and potential problems.

3. Encourage others, throughout their careers, to participate in professional activities and associations.

4. Allocate time to meet with students and provide a bridge between classroom studies and the realities of public service. Enforcement of the Code of Ethics shall be conducted in accordance with Article I, Section 4 of ASPA's Bylaws.

Sometimes Choices Can Be Difficult

They were rough on us in training. They would put us in difficult situations. Here's one: We had an important mission we had to complete. We had to blow up a bridge—in a hurry. If we did not do so and the enemy could cross the bridge, they would overwhelm and kill forty of our people defending a village. The bridge was across a mountain from us. We had a truck. We loaded the back of the truck with six men, their weapons, and explosive devices. Because of the urgency of time, the explosives were activated so that they could be quickly placed by the bridge and detonated. This meant we had to drive the truck very carefully. A rough shock could cause an explosion. I was the driver. It was night, but we could not use our headlights, because we might be seen. Reflections off of the moon gave us our only light.

The mountain road had many curves. On one side it had a ditch and then the side of the mountain. On the other side were dropoffs of several hundreds of feet. I had to drive as fast as I could under the circumstances. Margins for error were near zero. Sudden stops would be almost impossible to make, while the many curves on the mountain made gentle stops unlikely as well. As I was driving down the mountain, I negotiated a turn, and when I did so, I noticed an object in the road in front of me. In the moonlight I could see it was a child in the middle of the road directly in front of me.

This is an old training story (paraphrased) told to one author by G. Gordon Liddy. Liddy was addressing an assembly of college students at the University of Nevada–Las Vegas, September 17, 1984.

At this point the class instructor asked me what I would do. My mind quickly ran through the impossible alternatives. "Quickly, quickly, I need an answer," the instructor yelled.

As I was about to speak, the instructor made another statement.

"You are now almost on top of the child, and the child turns his face toward the moonlight. You see it is *your* little boy."

A Bitter Taste on the Lips

I had just spent six weeks in the wilderness. My job was to search for berries and plants that we could store for the winter. I had been all alone, and I was very much looking forward to my return to the village and human contact with others. I was very, very lonely. Our village was isolated. It was deep into the jungle. The closest neighboring village was over 2 months away on foot, and no one could make the trip alone. We could travel outward only in groups for visits to outside communities to get supplies, as we had to help each other ford the rivers and climb steep hills. With winter coming, such a trip even with a group would be nearly impossible. We would have to be a close knit community for several months.

As I approached the village I could see some of my friends. I yelled out in exuberance. My friends saw me, but they did not stop to return greetings. They just smiled and looked away paying me almost no attention at all. Then as I came closer, I saw my brother. I spoke to him and he heard, but his response seemed to be gibberish. I asked him what was happening. He spoke more gibberish and turned to others, and they spoke foolish nonsensical words to each other. I went to several people and asked what had happened. The responses were the same—nonresponses, foolish words, gibberish. I was hungry and I saw people eating. I went among them

This is an old story that was told to one author by University President Delyte Morris (deceased) at Southern Illinois University freshman orientation, 1958.

and reached for food. They smiled as I took food and ate. They smiled at me but acted as if they did not know me, and they made more nonsensical utterances.

I retreated and found a place where I could sit by myself and try to figure out what was happening. Then I noticed a waterfall that had been dry for over a year. It was gushing forth much water. There must have been a large storm. Then I noticed that the falls ran over the ground where the oil barrels were placed. A caravan had brought them months before, and they furnished us with the oil for our fires—fires we would need through the winter. The water that ran by the barrels also ran into the water storage tank. The tank was placed to gather rain waters that could be used for all purposes—bathing, cooking, and drinking. I noticed a young boy, my friend's son, come to the tank with a bucket, fill it up, and take it back to his hut. Then I saw an old man—it was my uncle—come to the tank with a ladle. He filled it and drank the water, and then he walked back toward the huts.

I went over by the tank. I could see that the water had a light film of oil on it. It was contaminated. The people had been drinking poisoned water. They were acting as if they all had schizophrenia, and there was a reason for their actions. Yet they were all getting along with each other, as if they were totally unaware of what was happening. They were totally unaware of what was happening. But they were content. They looked healthy otherwise. I quickly went around the edge of the village and I counted people. There were 47. That was the same number the village had when I had left. No one had died. No one appeared to be sick. They were peaceful, and from what I could observe they were happy. But they were flat out, out of their minds. Not a single one of them was sane.

I sat alone. I thought. I asked myself: should I drink the water?

Annotated Bibliography of Selected Books

Adams, Guy and Danny L. Balfour. *Unmasking Administrative Evil.* Armonk, NY: M. E. Sharpe, 2004.
Administrative evil has been overlooked in public administrative theory, yet it is a consequence of modern organization with its efficiency and with its professionalism. Adams and Balfour present case studies to illustrate the efficiency involved in the Nazi Holocaust, events at the National Atmospheric and Space Administration that were tied to the *Challenger* and *Columbia* disasters, as well as the Japanese-American relocation program of World War II. The authors lament that administrative rationality—often the lofty goal of public administration theory—is procedural and not substantive. To get to a quality of outputs requires a new kind of organization. That new organization should decry the arrogance of "a public ethics based on grand designs of human perfectibility" (p. 162) and admit instead to human frailty in organizations. With deliberate efforts and great vigilance, we can do better.

Bayles, Michael. *Professional Ethics.* 2nd ed. Belmont, CA: Wadsworth, 1989.
Professions are composed of large numbers of elites. They serve as leading decision makers in society and therefore should be considered as ethical role models for all citizens. Yet professions and professionals have been exposed for having many ethical flaws. This volume examines professional ethics by looking at obligations to both clients and the public. A concluding chapter offers measures for ensuring professional compliance with ethical standards, including internal professional controls

and self-regulation, codes of ethics, and professional motivations. Several case studies and problem situations are presented to the reader for consideration.

Bok, Sissela. *Lying: Moral Choice in Public and Private Life.* 3rd ed. New York: Vintage, 1999.
A father in the hospital on the edge of death inquires about his son who had been in a terrible accident. "Is he alive?" In fact, he is dead, and the doctors know this. But the doctors fear that news of his son's death will kill the father given his fragile condition. If they don't answer, the father will know. What should they say? Should they lie? Is it ever right to lie? When? Under what circumstances? In 1978, Sissela Bok put together the first contemporary analysis of the lie. She launches the first edition of her work with a theoretical treatment of what constitutes the truth. She then looks at literature from the distant past as she finds little or nothing in recent writings. She examines philosophical and religious treatments of lying and its consequences. In her subsequent editions of *Lying*, Bok acknowledges that the Vietnam-Watergate interlude had generated vast writings on the subject, but she held to repeating her earlier text in the second and third editions. The book offers chapters on excuses, white lies, lying to liars, lying to enemies, and lying for the public good. Her text is followed with passages from the writings of several leading authorities on the subject, including Augustine, Aquinas, Bacon, Kant, and Bonhoeffer.

Bowman, James S., and Frederick A. Elliston. *Ethics, Government, and Public Policy: A Reference Guide.* New York: Greenwood Press, 1988.
The authors present thirteen essays in four different sections: (1) analytical approaches to the study of ethics; (2) ethical standards and dilemmas for public actors; (3) methodologies for ethical decision making; and (4) studies of systemic issues in government. The authors do many things, including integrating several approaches to ethics such as personal, professional, and organizational; presenting historical overviews of literature in public ethic studies; relating individual ethics with organizational morality; discussing techniques and institutions for assuring ethical behaviors such as ombudsmen, risk analyses, negotiations, codes of ethics, and equal opportunity laws. The systemic issues examined include an analysis of waste fraud and abuse in administration. A concluding essay focuses upon a comparative analysis of ethics, public policy, and the public service.

Bowman, James S., and Donald C. Menzel, eds. *Teaching Ethics and Values in Public Administration Programs: Innovations, Strategies, and Issues.* Albany: State University of New York Press, 1998.
The editors explore the status of teaching of ethics in academic public administration programs in the United States. They find that a majority of programs teach specific ethics courses, yet they also find that the courses do not seem to make students more ethical. A review of teaching leads to the conclusion that ethics as a field of study needs much development. They seek to add to the development by bringing together a set of essays by sixteen public administration instructors. The essays give

fresh perspectives to be considered by all instructors. Innovative programs as well as new teaching strategies are explored.

Bruce, Willa, ed. *Classics of Administrative Ethics.* Boulder, CO: Westview Press, 2001.

For this book, Professor Bruce has selected twenty-nine essays that were first published by the American Society of Public Administration. They look at administrative responsibility from a theoretical perspective as well as provide guidelines for practical decision making. Several articles deal with corruption and scandals, others with codes of ethics and enforcement of ethical behavior. Attention is given to whistle-blowing and also to the concept of having inspector generals. Moral education and the public administrative curriculum are also examined, as is the notion of professionalism in public service employment. The essays are written by a collection of the most highly acclaimed scholars in the field of public administration, and collectively they give the reader a chance to grasp the essence of the nature of ethical issues in the public sector.

Cooper, Terry L. *The Responsible Administrator: An Approach to Ethics for the Administrative Role.* San Francisco: Jossey Bass, 1990.

While the National Association of Schools of Public Affairs and Administration implores its members to enhance values, knowledge, and skills in order to act ethically, ethics studies are hardly a fad. Terry Cooper's book is a response to his perceived need to fill a void by concentrating on ethical decision making. First he presents a step-by-step model integrating moral rules, ethical principles, and norms. His second chapter looks at the social context of decisions. He follows this by examining organizational roles as well as controls such as those provided by codes of ethics, ethics legislation, and professional values. There is also consideration given to authority structures and personal autonomy. Several case studies appear throughout the chapters.

Denhardt, Kathryn G. *The Ethics of Public Service: Resolving Moral Dilemmas in Public Organizations.* Westport, CT: Greenwood Press, 1988.

Author Kathryn Denhardt laments the absence of a consensus regarding what is ethical administrative behavior. Therefore she sets upon the task of laying the groundwork for a theory from which a consensus may follow. In doing so, she offers an in-depth discussion of theories extant in the literature of public administration, tying them to the social and historical context of the field, as well as its organizational and individual contexts. The approach is then examined with its application to a real-life case study.

Dobel, J. Patrick. *Public Integrity.* Baltimore, MD: Johns Hopkins University Press, 1999.

Integrity is formulated in individuals before they come into office. Ethics is personnel. The focus of Dobel's book is on the individual and situations surrounding individuals. Public discretion in office is an interactive process involving ties between obligations of the office, one's personal commitments, and effectiveness in job performance. As these matters inevitably come into conflict, integrity builds upon a personal morality that requires efforts and sacrifice. Chapters reflect on the temptations of power, character development, commitment to one's office, the ethics of resigning from office, and how private lives are related to public purpose. The author uses skill in tying case studies with literature and films in his chapter discussions.

Donahue, Anne Marie, ed. *Ethics in Politics and Government.* New York: H.W. Wilson, 1989.
Eighteen essays present ideas from leading public officials and commentators as well as scholars and authors. The focus is broad, covering foreign policy, White House affairs, Congress, political campaigns, and general considerations of leadership and individual character.

Frederickson, H. George, ed. *Ethics in Public Administration.* Armonk, NY: M.E. Sharpe, 1993.
The editor postulates that the development of modern public administration was a reaction to perceived corruption in government a century ago. Then, reforms concentrated on government procedures and structures. Today, a reaction to corruption has produced a government ethics movement. The movement shall be sustained by the widespread prevalence of contemporary corruption at all levels of government, by the fact that the public is very aware of corruption due to expanded media, by controls becoming more institutionalized, and by the fact that ethics affects all sectors of society, not just government. The book presents thirteen essays that consider the wide expanse of ethical problems in government as well as issues such as the value of codes of ethics, inspectors general, and whistle-blowing.

Frederickson, H. George, and Richard K. Ghere, eds. *Ethics in Public Management.* Armonk, NY: M.E. Sharpe, 2005.
This is a collection of seventeen essays that look at normative foundations for ethical studies of administration, organizational design, market force factors, and concerns for social justice. Several chapters explore and debate the politics–administrative dichotomy and whether separate or conjoined politics in administration promote ethical behavior or not. The notions of a technically rational bureaucracy are also challenged from an ethical perspective. Several essays also focus upon contemporary problems emerging from the American military confrontation in Iraq and Afghanistan. The book concludes with essays discussing whether ethical norms in the United States may be easily fit into a global context.

Garofalo, Charles, and Dean Geuras. *Ethics in the Public Service: The Moral Mind at Work.* Washington, DC: Georgetown University Press, 1999.
The authors are very critical of public administration practitioners and scholars for not establishing an ethical foundation in their work. Special dismay is held for the

Minnowbrook groups, which advanced a new public administration in which bureaucrats would take a societal lead in policy formulation and decision making. The groups did not offer moral criteria on which good decisions could be made. The authors review in depth several theories of ethics, but reject the notion that any one theoretical set can be sufficient for administrators. Instead they offer their own model, which brings unity to four theories: deontology (Kant), teleology (Bentham), character-based (Plato), and intuitionist (Moore).

Glazer, Myron P., and Penina M. Glazer. *The Whistleblowers: Exposing Corruption in Government and Industry.* New York: Basic Books, 1989.
For 6 years the authors traveled about the United States seeking persons they called "ethical resisters," persons also known as whistle-blowers. They interviewed them attempting to find why some people are willing to disobey superiors and expose wrongdoing in their organizations. The authors also explain the consequences of these people's actions. The book also looks at whistle-blowing as a movement with origins in societal disillusionment with the Vietnam War and the Watergate scandal. The book concludes by showing the importance of professional organizations in supporting employees who risk careers in revealing unwelcome truths to the public. The authors list organizations that may help whistle-blowers.

Gortner, Harold F. *Ethics for Public Managers.* Westport, CT: Greenwood Press, 1991.
The public administrator must deal with wicked and tragic issues. These are situations that cannot have win-win solutions. Because of scarce resources, someone has to lose. They also encompass complex situations that defy definition. Ethical dilemmas follow. In Gortner's analysis of ethics, he postulates a five-sided model for seeking explanations. The actor must consider (1) self-evaluation, personality factors, and mixtures of self-interest and altruism; (2) the law surrounding decisions, (3) the societal culture and factors such as expectation of trust and personal autonomy, (4) organizational dynamics including growth cycles and power structures, and (5) professionalism. In a concluding chapter, the author brings together the five factors as he presents criteria for analyzing specific ethical dilemmas.

Heller, Joseph. *Catch 22: A Novel.* New York: Simon and Schuster, 1961.
This is the quintessential novel about dilemmas (ethical and all other kinds) presented in organizational life. The absurdity of bureaucracy pervades each of the episodes that takes place among a World War II squadron of Army Air Force personnel on a Mediterranean island. Catch 22 refers to the hopeless no-win situations facing squadron members—especially bombardier John Yossarian—from the onset to the finish. *Logical irrationality* is a phrase applied to the organizational existence of the men. A theme of the book is that without checks and balances, rules take on a life of their own and dominate all other matters of life. The only way to survive in an insane world seems to be to become insane yourself. (See Appendix III.)

Knowles, Jeffrey J. *Integrity with Two Eyes: An Insider's Slant on the Moral Climate of Government*. Lanham, MD: University Press of America, 1999.

Jeffrey Knowles was a state government bureaucrat for 25 years. He finds that the public service can be reformed and improved only if those improvements are tied closely to integrity. "The real potential for good government is as deep, or as shallow, as our capacity to pursue integrity as a guiding principle . . . and to honor it for its own merits" (p. vi). Three steps stand before us as we begin reform: (1) understanding where we are, or perspective; (2) individually knowing where one stands in the bureaucracy, or placement; and (3) having a "clear and meaningful sense of purpose" (p. 101). Using these three guideposts, Knowles offers ten chapters that reflect his personal quest for change in one department of a state government. His last chapter offers stages for an action plan, including: (1) pilot tests for allowing agency autonomy, (2) contract obligations for the agency, (3) a study of virtue, (4) using a code of ethics, (5) having multiple points of responsibility, (6) developing a citizen rating index, (7) rewriting the state's ethics law, (8) having an agency to evaluate other agencies, (9) pursuing the concept of choice in service delivery, and (10) having a task force study how integrity can be institutionalized in state government.

Menzel, Donald C. *Ethics Management for Public Administrators—Building Organizations of Integrity*. Armonk, New York: M.E. Sharpe, 2007.

This book has been written for students as well as administrators. It is essentially a how-to book that has as its goal the construction of organizational entities that incorporate integrity into their very fabric. *Ethics Management for Public Administrators* includes a thorough discussion of constitutional issues, an examination of the administrative environment surrounding the daily activity of bureaucrats, as well as descriptions of actual ethics development programs in place in local governments in America. The book also looks out at the national scene, reviewing major ethics legislation passed by Congress as well as executive directives and court cases at the national level. There is also a discussion of programs around the world. Each chapter of the book includes practical hands-on skill-building exercises that can be incorporated into either classroom teaching or workshops for administrators.

Pasquerella, Lynn, Alfred G. Killilea, and Michael Vocino, eds. *Ethical Dilemmas in Public Administration*. Westport, CT: Praeger, 1966.

The editors present ten essays that contain critical analyses of actual case dilemmas that have faced public administrations. These are preceded and followed by two theoretical pieces that place the dilemmas in the context of the classical thought of Niccolo Machiavelli as well as more contemporary observers. The final piece emphasizes a need to rediscover the public by placing the community back into decision-making endeavors. However, efforts for public participation need to be genuine and institutional rather than ad hoc window dressing. The cases look at issues such as a college using secrecy and dummy corporations to acquire land for development; a hospital's misdiagnoses of cancers and its cover-ups; confidentiality and the HIV status of a client of a drug abuse program; an F.B.I. inquiry into book circulation at a public library; the conflict between the need for control and inmate dignity at a women's prison; public employees who have political influence and engage in falsehoods regarding their work histories; illegal agency practices in a federally-funded social service program; mixing of roles as an administrator and legislator; the sludge disposal plans of a prison and the surrounding community; and dealing with budget cuts and fulfilling program obligations.

Riordon, William. *Plunkitt of Tammany Hall.* Boston: Bedford Books of St. Martin's Press, 1994.

George Washington Plunkitt was a New York assemblyman and leader in the Tammany Hall political organization for several decades in the late nineteenth century. He was a straight organization man who believed in party government without hypocrisy. Loyalty to party was among his highest values. William Riordan retrieved a series of Plunkitt's talks from various sources. The talks offer an honest view of ethics from one point of view. The talks have been widely distributed as evidence of a morality of the past, but may be very instructive for those dealing with administrative decision making today. Plunkitt distinguished honest graft (seeing your opportunities and taking them) from dishonest graft (simple stealing). He cursed Civil Service reform for taking incentives away from participation in politics. He saw the start of political careers in winning the allegiances of one other individual. Deals were reciprocal obligations. He adhered to the notions of Bentham: he sought the greatest good for the greatest number, and his eyes were always on the prize—the ends, whatever the manner.

Rohr, John A. *Ethics for Bureaucrats: An Essay on Law and Values.* New York: Marcel Decker, 1978.

John Rohr rejects the Wilsonian notion that bureaucrats can be removed from politics. Precisely because they are politicians, it becomes essential that they adhere to democratic values by acting in the public interest. This is their ethical duty. Even bureaucrats whose actions reflect routine processes must link their activity to the grand principles of the Republic. Bureaucrats take an oath to support the Constitution, and accordingly should always support the constitutional regime of the United States. His discussion leads to an explanation of critical regime values that should serve as ethical foundations for bureaucrats, including respect for law, the quest for equity, basic freedom of speech and religion, and the right to have and enjoy property. In actions, bureaucrats must be mindful of the activity of the Supreme Court in interpreting in the Constitution.

Steinberg, Sheldon S., and David T. Austern. *Government, Ethics, and Managers: A Guide to Solving Ethical Dilemmas in the Public Sector.* New York: Quorum Books, 1990.

The authors lament that the public is disenchanted with corruption at all levels of government, and that this presents a problem for effective government. Their first chapters are devoted to a recitation of case after case of wrongdoing and surveys of public discontentment. Case problems are presented for the reader to consider. A middle chapter presents three model profiles of public managers, including:

1. The no ethic corrupter, who has behaviors that are disconnected with any commitment to moral values. They tolerate corruption in others and do not avoid being in positions where their own activity may be compromised.
2. The valueless or relativistic functionary, who is neutral on ethical matters. While these persons may avoid being in compromising situations, they willingly close their eyes to corrupt activity by others.
3. The value-based ethicist, who actively avoids corrupting situations and is willing to intervene to prevent others from engaging in unethical situations, even to the extent of becoming an active whistle-blower.

Later chapters offer an ethics checklist and the four essentials of ethical practices in government: (1) training, (2) auditing, (3) investigations, and (4) management controls.

Svara, James. *Ethics Primer for Public Administration in Government and Nonprofit Organizations.* Sudbury, MA: Jones and Bartlett Publishers, 2007.
James Svara offers the readers a cogent overview of ethical responsibilities and challenges in public service and nonprofit management. He offers concise, meaningful discussions of codes of ethics, the activity of whistle-blowing and its consequences, how different types of administrators approach ethical dilemmas, and external measures to guard organizations against unethical practices. Appendices include standards of conduct and codes of ethics and an organizational ethical climate survey. The original key offering of the book that serves as a guide for discussion throughout is its ethical triangle. Svara postulates that duty to serve the public interest may be discerned when decision makers surround their issue of concern with: considerations of principles (justice, fairness, equity); notions of virtue and intuition (character); and consideration of the greatest good (consequences). Historical foundations are provided as each leg of the triangle is explained by delving into theories derived from Emanuel Kant, Aristotle and Plato, and Jeremy Bentham and John Stuart Mill. The authors of this case book have used Svara's triangle as a launching point for discussions of each case study presented.

Timmins, William M. *A Casebook of Public Ethics and Issues.* Pacific Grove, CA: Brooks/Cole, 1990.
Seventeen case study chapters are presented. Each real-life situation includes an introduction and ethical issue with details, along with assignments for student discussion. All have been used in the classroom. Cases examine issues such as drug testing in the workplace, catching an employee in a lie, salaries and comparable worth, mandatory employee fitness programs, problems with downsizing and privatizing, exchanging gifts, and smoking in the workplace.

Tong, Rosemary. *Ethics in Policy Analysis.* Englewood Cliffs, NJ: Prentice Hall, 1986.

Rosemary Tong's book focuses upon the role of policy analysts in government. At the beginning she offers the case study of budget director David Stockman and his advice to President Reagan regarding tax policy in 1981. In the process of supporting a major tax cut, Stockman came to discover numbers that revealed major flaws in the policy desired. What should he have done? In following chapters Tong indicates that policy directives must always be based upon a blurring of facts and values. She explores the role of the expert vis-à-vis the role of the citizen, and how reliance on expertise can generate citizen apathy. Institutions of policy making are examined as impediments to personal responsibility. She concludes with discussions about specific obligations that analysts owe to their clients, as well as to the general public.

West, Jonathan, and Evan Berman, eds. *The Ethics Edge.* 2nd ed. Washington, DC: ICMA, 2006.

The Ethics Edge is a compilation of essays published by the International City/County Management Association. The articles are focused in four component areas: (1) foundations, (2) leadership, (3) ethical management, and (4) ethical challenges. The authors also discuss a range of relevant topics, political sensitivities, habitual use of deceit and lies in administration, efforts to measure ethical behaviors, simple corruption, incompetence, and the public cynicism that follows. The challenges facing governments that seek to privatize operations are also given attention. This is one of the best collections of recent commentary on ethics in government.

A Selected List
of Films on Ethics

A Bridge Too Far (1977)

War is hell. Things happen. When leaders make bad decisions, people die. During the later stages of World War II (September 1944), British commanders in Operation Market Garden placed 35,000 paratroopers behind German lines in order to secure and preserve a collection of bridges and hold them for advancing ground troops. They miscalculated in an exuberance of impending victory, and the bridge at Arnhem, Netherlands, was lost. The film reveals that several leaders among those planning the attacks knew they did not have the resources for victory. They forecast defeat but their voices were not heard.

A Civil Action (1998)

A John Travolta film finds the actor playing a lawyer leading a class action suit against an industrial polluter. The film exposes good and bad motives of the plaintiffs and deception of the corporate defendants. As the case unfolds, the cost burdens on Travolta's character's firm rise considerably. The firm faces financial ruin. Travolta's character becomes more susceptible to meeting the defendant's offers for a settlement only to be stonewalled as both greed and honor afflict the victims of the company's pollution.

Class Action (1991)

This film presents an interesting combination of a father opposing his daughter as rival attorneys in civil litigation involving product liability of an automaker. The father, played by Gene Hackman, represents a plaintiff who was involved in an accident. The daughter's law firm represents the car maker charged with using faulty equipment on the vehicles they make. In the course of the case, the daughter discovers the corporation's deceptions and her partners' cover-ups and lies. Although she has serious father–daughter relationship issues, she seeks an ethical way to let her father know the truth.

Codebreakers (2005)

The motto of the U.S. Military Academy at West Point is, "Duty, honor, country." An academy cadet never lies, cheats, or tolerates those who do. However, members of the 1951 championship football team were under tremendous stress to perform well both on the field and in the classroom. As some instructors used the same examination in multiple sections of the same course (meeting at different times), players developed a scheme for passing exam questions on to other players before they would have to sit for the exams. Others became aware of the scheme even though they did not participate, and they faced the dilemmas of being code violators simply by being aware. In this true-life story, one cadet felt obligated to inform academy authorities, not knowing what the consequences would be. As a result, over half of the football team was dismissed from the academy even though many had not participated in using the questions. Issues of honor are juxtaposed with questions about loyalties—to fellow cadets, to the academy, and to the code.

The Doctor (1991)

William Hurt portrays an arrogant doctor operating in an uncaring hospital organization. Hurt's character constantly invokes humor at the expense of troubled and ailing patients. He chides a breast cancer victim concerned about her husband's affections by saying, "Tell him you are a *Playboy* centerfold. You have the staples to prove it." He supports bureaucratic bungling and even malpractice by his partners. He hides the truth from patients. Then he is diagnosed with throat cancer. He becomes a patient in his own uncaring hospital. Life roles are changed. As we see him progress (or not progress) through treatment side by side with other patients, we find his mind-set being altered. He comes to embrace the need for truth. He refuses to help his partners lie in a lawsuit. He understands the purpose of the hospital is not to help the egos of rich doctors, but rather to help patients.

The Fountainhead (1949)

A film based upon an Ayn Rand novel shows the conflict between an individual trying to be true to his personal values in the face of overwhelming group pressures pulling him in another direction. The protagonist is a young architect who envisions new styles in his buildings. His clients love what he gives them, but they ask him to make changes so that the buildings will conform with accepted standards of the day. He resists to the point of facing financial ruin. Yet he persists, and in the end he is vindicated for his innovations.

Good Night and Good Luck (2005)

This film presents the story of television journalist Edward R. Murrow as he engages in combat with Senator Joseph McCarthy and the senator's witch hunt against mostly imagined-to-be Communists in our midst. Murrow has to confront his bosses at CBS television and stand his ground lest they silence him for airing dissent and inviting criticism from a shy public and wary sponsors. Murrow survives the battles to witness the eventual downfall of the senator and his misguided campaigns.

High Noon (1952)

All that is necessary for evil to triumph is for good men to do nothing. The 1952 western *High Noon* offers a setting for reflection upon this John Stuart Mill truism. The town marshal has just married a pacifist and he has promised to resign his law enforcement job. However, on his wedding day, an outlaw comes to town with his gang seeking revenge against the marshal. Townspeople tell him to leave, and his wife says she will leave even if he does not. No one in town indicates a willingness to stand with him against the outlaws. He has his duty. Alone, he faces four gunmen. In the end, his wife joins him and from cover shoots one of the outlaws in the back. She has chosen her husband's life over her religious principles.

Little Miss Sunshine (2006)

Little Miss Sunshine exposes all the dirty linen of the dysfunctional Hoover family— but it exposes more as well. A father has pinned life hopes on a book he has written about winners and losers. However, he confronts a callous hypocrisy from the publishing industry—he has a great book, but the problem is he is not already a recognized author. A 15-year-old son dreams to be a fighter pilot and goes into total seclusion as he passes time waiting for admission to the Air Force Academy. An uncle who is retrieved from a hospital following a suicide attempt is totally disillusioned with a gay love affair gone bad and his losses in the academic jungle to more sophisticated scholars. Grandpa is on cocaine as he trains his 7-year-old granddaughter in her talent routines for a beauty pageant—à la JonBenet Ramsey. A realistic mother seeks to hold things together as the family travels from Albuquerque to Redondo Beach in a Volkswagen bus for the pageant. The film exposes the hypocrisy and bad taste of child beauty pageants with supreme satire. *Little Miss Sunshine* shines with a simulated pornographic dance. At the end, truth triumphs and an intact family leaves California with an acceptance of life's reality.

Lord of War (2005)

Nicolas Cage portrays Russian immigrant Yuri Orlov in his rise from near-poverty to untold wealth as an arms merchant. His journey begins and ends with deceit as he manipulates his family, lies to his wife and parents, and engages in transactions with dictators who could be described as genocidal maniacs. He takes no sides and sells guns to anyone as he lives by his own rules: never get shot by your own merchandise, be sure to get paid, never join with your customers, and never go to war.

When he is finally captured by justice officials for illegal gun sales, he is soon set free because of the interactions of higher political authorities who need his services for certain sales that cannot be made by good people. By then, however, he has been rejected and disowned by his family and friends. The film attempts to expose the governments of the Unites States and other Security Council countries as the world's top gun merchants. Orlov is just small potatoes in the big scheme of things.

On the Waterfront (1954)

This drama about loyalty and violence in the longshoreman's union stars Marlon Brando. He is the favored character of the union boss who gives him choice jobs but expects much in return—his services as a thug when his fists are needed. He reluctantly accepts his role as he has failed in trying to launch a boxing career—due to the fact that the boss made him take a fall so he could win big bets. He unwittingly tips off the boss about the whereabouts of a friend who has crossed the boss. He thinks the friend may be beaten up, but the friend is murdered. The Brando character realizes how he has been used. He soon meets his friend's sister. Brando's character gradually turns against his boss, although his brother, a union attorney, begs him to stay away from authorities investigating union corruption. The union misreads the brother's intentions and he is murdered. Brando's character realizes that his loyalties must be with his new love and with his brother's memory. He goes to the authorities and testifies against his boss.

Philadelphia (1993)

A young attorney with a leading Philadelphia law firm develops visible symptoms of AIDS. The firm uses deception and contrived evidence to justify removing the lawyer from cases and then firing him for incompetence. The young lawyer seeks counsel but is repeatedly turned down. Finally he finds someone to represent him, and he files a case for wrongful dismissal. The case is successful, but by the time it has gone through trial phases, the young lawyer is in the hospital in the last days of his life.

The Player (1992)

This film takes an unflattering look at Hollywood executives and the way they treat potential screenwriters. One studio vice president's callous rejection procedures earn him death threats. The plot evolves with confrontations, rage, and a perhaps "accidental" killing, followed by cover-ups, lies, and more deception.

Pork Chop Hill (1959)

This war story concentrates on one of the most brutal series of battles during the Korean War (1950–1953). The vicious fighting takes place during a time of cease fire negotiations. The combat operations are basically senseless as the parties behind the forces know that they will soon have an agreement, and they are only interested in political posturing rather than military objectives. In the end, the U.S./U.N. forces withdraw from their positions and yield Pork Chop Hill to the Communists. The cease fire then begins.

Quiz Show (1994)

The film is based upon 1950s television quiz shows. As one show, *21*, began to win top ratings, its producers decided to control the drama by preparing the contestants with answers to the questions. They coached a respected university professor from a family of renowned scholars to be their model of brilliance. Their ratings soared until a rival contestant who was not included in the new rules of the game suspected that the show was rigged. But was the show just entertainment? If the public loved it, did it matter? A congressional investigation suggested it did matter.

Remains of the Day (1993)

Anthony Hopkins portrays an English butler whose life has been dedicated to the service of his wealthy boss, a lord of the realm. As his life is coming toward its end, he reflects upon his moral worth. He was loyal to his boss, even when he had to choose between his boss and his father. He was loyal to his boss, even though his boss was a Nazi sympathizer. In doing his duty, the butler had obeyed orders that he knew were morally wrong. He fired a young servant who was Jewish for that reason alone. Without employment, the servant was returned to Europe, portions of which were under Nazi rule. Yet while the butler had done his job very well, he came to believe that he should change the course of his life and allow his own feelings to be involved in his service to a new boss, an American with a much more democratic posture in life.

Roger and Me (1989)

Michael Moore's first documentary-exposé reveals the callous nature of large corporations (this time General Motors) as they downsize operations and move facilities to other countries. Moore's hometown of Flint, Michigan is victimized as auto-making factories are closed and General Motors opens new plants in Mexico. The corporation is shown as uncaring about the community it leaves behind. The theme is cleverly offered with dramatic realism that belies total veracity. An issue with the film is how the filmmaker manipulated scenes with changed time sequences and out-of-context conclusions.

Shattered Glass (2003)

The film offers the true story of Stephen Glass. As a young journalist in his 20s with high academic credentials, Glass seeks shortcuts to the top. As editor of his university newspaper, he writes an exposé of the United Way. This propels him into a job with the *New Republic*. There he thrives with exposé after exposé. He writes forty-one articles before a rival magazine writer challenges his sources. Quickly, Glass becomes the subject of the story as he is demonstrated to have created a litany of lies to hold his stories together. Of his forty-one stories, twenty-seven are based on discovered falsehoods, while doubts remain about the others. Glass is fired. Ethical questions about institutions persist. After all his overt cheating is revealed, he is admitted as a student of Georgetown Law School, and he finds a major publisher willing to publish his memoirs, which many believe contain further fabrications. Unlike the author in *Little Miss Sunshine*, he is already a recognized author.

Super Size Me (2004)

This documentary film dramatically reveals the dangers and the deceit rampant in promotions of the fast food industry. The main character embarks in a health-destroying 30-day experiment during which he eats every meal at a McDonald's restaurant. As the last days of the experiment unwind, doctors urge him to quit as they see serious deterioration in his health. They fear permanent damage. He is able to survive, but in a year's time he has still not returned to his previous levels of good health. As a result of the film, the fast food chains have sought to upgrade their images by offering some healthful food choices. Or are their changes only facades?

That Championship Season (1982)

Loyalty and deceit, political incompetence and corruption, hypocrisy and the rules of the game, small city bigotry—all these factors weave together in this Broadway play transformed to the big screen. The 1982 film, *That Championship Season* exhibits the interactions among four members of the 1957 Pennsylvania state championship high school basketball team and their coach as they come together for a twenty-fourth reunion celebration of their victory. One starting team member is the bumbling city mayor locked into what is sure to be a losing reelection campaign. The second is his main financial sponsor—an affluent businessman dependent upon contracts given by the city. The third is a junior high school principal lost in the despair of a mid-life crisis, while the fourth is the principal's alcoholic brother, a loser who has fallen through the cracks in life's race. The fifth starting team member refuses to associate with the group. Life's dirty secrets come out in their alcohol-induced interactions, as their revered coach is revealed to have engaged in dirty tactics on the road to their great victory, and as they scheme to scrape the moral bottom planning the mayor's reelection.

Wall Street (1987)

Actor Michael Douglas portrays Wall Street wheeler-dealer Gordon Gekko. Gekko thrives on spying and gaining inside information in order to structure financial deals. He takes on a young protégé, Bud Fox, played by Charlie Sheen. Fox admires Gekko, his expensive tastes, and his fast lifestyle. Gekko uses Fox to gain inside information about a company that employs Fox's father. Fox compromises loyalty to his father and delivers the information. With inside secrets, Gekko acts as Fox never thought he would, taking over the company and dismantling the plant where Fox's father works. Fox feels betrayed. Authorities investigating Gekko learn of the protégé's feelings and approach him with a request to turn on his idol.

Index

A

Absenteeism, in public sector employment, 46
Academic articles, plagiarism and, 45–48
Adams, Guy, 153
Adler, Felix, 57
Administrative evil, 153
Air conditioning retrofitting, apartment fire and, 61–62
Alcoholism, history of, building inspector and, 65–66
American Society for Public Administration, 155
    Code of Ethics, 146–147
        demonstrate personal integrity, 147
        promote ethical organizations, 147–148
        respect the Constitution and the law, 147
        serve the public interest, 146
        strive for professional excellence, 148
Annexation actions, 111–115
Apartment fire, revealing truth about, 61–62
Appointment commitment, ICMA guidelines, 140
Aquinas, Thomas, 154
Aristotle, 160
Armour, Paul, 74
Arrests, for solicitation, 85, 87
Asimov, Isaac, 1
ASPA Code of Ethics. *See* American Society for Public
    Administration Code of Ethics
Assessment dispute, 105–109
Assessor examinations, 106
Audits, 28
Augustine (saint), 154
Austern, David T., 159

B

Bacon, Francis, 154
Balfour, Danny L., 153
Bayles, Michael, 153
Bentham, Jeremy, 157, 160
Berman, Evan, 161
Bids
    for sewer construction, 32, 33
    for street construction, 26
Bizarre behavior at work, official reaction to, 41–42
Block grants, 25, 26
Boetcker, William J. H., 25
Bok, Sissela, 154
Bonds, sewer construction and, 32

Bonhoeffer, Dietrich, 154
Bowman, James S., 154
Brando, Marlon, 166
Bridge Too Far, A (film), 163
Brontë, Charlotte, 11
Bruce, Willa, 155
Buck, Pearl, 83
Buddha, 39
Budgets, training, 80–81
Building inspection, apartment fire and case of
    nonfeasance related to, 62
Building inspectors
    hiring of, 63–66
    retirement of, 62–63
Burke, Edmund, 111
Burnout, 74
Business personal property, taxes and, 94, 96

C

Cage, Nicolas, 165
Career changers, C.E.T.A. and, 131
Casebook of Public Ethics and Issues, A (Timmins), 160
Catch 22: A Novel (Heller), 36, 157
Categorical grant programs, 130
Cemetery land purchase, 113–115
C.E.T.A. *See* Comprehensive Employment Training
    Administration
Challenger disaster, 153
Character-based theory, 157
Child abuse, Munchausen syndrome by proxy and,
    120–126
Children, sidewalk project and safety of, 1–5
Churning, 80
Cicero, 73
Citizen complaints, about policemen, 36
City Confidential (television show), 118
City manager
    ethical lapses of, 19–23
    trusting instincts and hiring process for chief of
        police by, 11–17
City vehicle use, leaves of absence and, 14
City-wide renovations, 20
Civil Action, A (film), 163
Civil defense directorship, tornado and, 75, 77
Civil Service Commission, 40
Civil service system, 40

Class Action (film), 163–164
Classics of Administrative Ethics (Bruce), 155
Clerical jobs, growing of, into professional positions, 103
Codebreakers (film), 164
Codes of ethics, 139–148
    American Society for Public Administration, 146–148
    International City/County Management Association, 139–146
Collective bargaining contract, police force, mayor on city's bargaining team and, 8–9
Columbia disaster, 153
Community development grants, irregularities in use of, 26–27
Competence, 73, 74
Comprehensive Employment and Training Act of 1973, basic premise of, 130–131
Comprehensive Employment Training Administration
    ex-convicts and hiring procedures for, 4–5
    police cadet program and, 133
    real estate agent turned police officer and, 131–133
    sewer construction and, 33–34
    sidewalk project and hiring procedures for, 3–4
    wandering firefighter and, 135–137
Confidential information, ICMA guidelines and, 141, 145
Conflicts of interest, ICMA guidelines and, 145
Congress (U.S.), sewer construction in rural communities and funds appropriated by, 31
Constitution, American Society for Public Administration Code of Ethics and respect for, 147
Construction materials examination, for building inspectors, 64
Cooper, Terry L., 155
Corruption, reaction to, 156
Cost basis evaluations, for assessments, 106
Cost-of-living raises, 81
Council-manager plan, ICMA guidelines on elections and, 143
Credentials
    ICMA guidelines on, 140
    lies about, 20, 21
Crime, in impoverished city area, 12

D

Demotions, of police officers, 135
Denhardt, Kathryn G., 155
Deontology, 157
Difficult choices, 149–150
Dirty jobs, dumping of, on new people, 33–34
Disabilities, on-duty traffic accident and, 57–59
Disciplinary actions, against city manager, 21
Discretion, 69, 88, 89
Discriminatory hiring practices, in police department, 12
Disloyalty, 80
Divorce, 65
Dobel, J. Patrick, 155

Doctor, The (film), 164
Domestic violence calls, 41
Donahue, Anne Marie, 156
Douglas, Michael, 168
Drug dependency, 88–90
Drug trafficking, 133–134
Drunk driver, illegal detainment of, 36–37

E

Educational credentials, lies about, 20, 21
Effectiveness, 73
Efficiency, 73
Einstein, Albert, 61
Elected officials, ethics of, 83–90
Elections
    ICMA guidelines on, 142–143
    mayoral, loyalty to electorate and, 7–8
Elective office, felons and eligibility for, 84–85
Electrical examination, for building inspectors, 64
Eliot, T. S., 99
Elites, 153
Elliston, Frederick A., 154
Emergency declarations, 76
Employment, ICMA guidelines on seeking of, 141
Endorsements, ICMA guidelines and, 146
Environmental Protection Agency, 32
Equal opportunity, ICMA guidelines on, 144
Ericson, Edward, 45
Ethical behavior, moral principles of, 83–90
Ethical Dilemmas in Public Administration (Pasquerella, Killilea, and Vocino), 158
Ethical organizations, personal, American Society for Public Administration Code of Ethics and promotion of, 147–148
Ethical resisters, 157
Ethical standards, for elected officials vs. for appointed officials, 83
Ethics
    annotated bibliography of books on, 153–161
    of elected officials, 83–90
    films on, 163–168
Ethics, Government, and Public Policy: A Reference Guide (Bowman and Elliston), 154
Ethics Edge, The (West and Berman), 161
Ethics for Bureaucrats: An Essay on Law and Values (Rohr), 159
Ethics for Public Managers (Gortner), 157
Ethics in Policy Analysis (Tong), 161
Ethics in Politics and Government (Donahue), 156
Ethics in Public Administration (Frederickson), 156
Ethics in Public Management (Frederickson and Ghere), 156–157
Ethics in the Public Service: The Moral Mind at Work (Garofalo and Geuras), 156
Ethics Management for Public Administrators—Building Organizations of Integrity (Menzel), 158
Ethics of Public Service, The: Resolving Moral Dilemmas in Public Organizations (Denhardt), 155

Ethics Primer for Public Administration in Government and Nonprofit Organizations (Svara), 160
Ethics violations, ICMA guidelines on reporting of, 141
Excellence
in local governance, mission of ICMA and, 139
professional, American Society for Public Administration Code of Ethics and, 148

F

Family leave requests, 14
Family Medical Leave Act, 119
Federal aid, after tornado, 76
Federal deficit, 130
Federal revenue sharing program, 129–130
Felons, eligibility for elective office and, 84–85
Films, on ethics, 163–168
Fire fighter, termination of, 136, 137
Fire in building, air conditioning retrofitting, building inspection and, 61–62
Fire infrastructure, development of, in urbanized township, 93
Fire services, ten-mill tax for, 94, 96
Fire stations, 35
Firings
of city manager, 20–21
disability related to on-duty traffic accident and, 57–59
patronage appointees and, 101
of police chief, 17
of police officer, 133
FMLA. *See* Family Medical Leave Act
Forensic Files (television show), 118
48 Hours (television show), 118
Fountainhead, The (film), 164
4-day Kelly, 135
"Four Way Test" (Taylor), 93
Fraud, 26
Frederickson, H. George, 156
Friendships, hiring decisions and, 102

G

Garofalo, Charles, 156
General Motors, 167
George Washington Plunkitt, 100
Geuras, Dean, 156
Ghere, Richard K., 156
Gifts, ICMA guidelines on, 144
Glass, Stephen, 167
Glazer, Myron P., 157
Glazer, Penina M., 157
Good Night and Good Luck (film), 165
Gortner, Harold F., 157
Governing body, ICMA guidelines on elections of, 142
Government, Ethics, and Managers: A Guide to Solving Ethical Dilemmas in the Public Sector (Steinberg and Austern), 159–160
Graft, "honest," 26
Grant programs, irregularities in, 25–26

Grant proposals, 25
Great Depression, 130
Grievance settlement document, for fire fighter, 137
Gun merchants, 165–166

H

Hackman, Gene, 164
Heller, Joseph, 36, 157
High Noon (film), 165
Hiring
C.E.T.A., of real estate agent turned police officer, 131–133
civil service system for, 40
discriminatory practices in, for police department, 12
friendships and decisions about, 102
laws of God vs. laws of men and, 5
for recreation program, 79
Holocaust, 153
Homeowners, sidewalk project and opposition by, 2, 3
Homicides, 12, 40, 42
Hopkins, Anthony, 167
Hostage crisis, 70
Hull, Raymond, 73, 74
Hurt, William, 164

I

ICMA, essays published by, 161
ICMA Code of Ethics, 139–146
advice to officials of other local governments, 140
appointment commitment, 140
confidential information, 145
confidentiality, 141
conflicting roles, 142
credentials, 140
elections, 142–143
elections of elected executives, 142
elections of the governing body, 142
elections on the council-manager plan, 143
employment seeking, 141
endorsements, 146
equal opportunity, 144
gifts, 144
ICMA mission, 139
impression of influence, 140
information sharing, 144
investments in conflict with official duties, 145
length of service, 141
personal relationships, 145
presentation of issues, 143
private employment, 145
professional development, 143
professional respect, 140–141
public confidence, 140
reporting ethics violations, 141
representation, 145
running for office, 142
self-assessment, 143

Incest, 70
Income approach, in assessment, 106
Incompetence, 73, 74, 79, 85
  of elected officials, 84
  Peter case and, 75
Incurable diseases, 119–120
Inflation, 32
Influence, ICMA guidelines and impression of, 140
Information sharing, ICMA guidelines on, 144
Infrastructure capital, federal revenue sharing program
  and, 129–130
Input requirements of the job, 73, 74
Insider information, misuse of, 70–71
Instinct, trusting, hiring process for chief of police
  and, 11–17
Insurance ratings, apartment fire damages and
  potential adverse consequences of, 62
Integrity, personal, American Society for Public
  Administration Code of Ethics and, 147
*Integrity with Two Eyes: An Insider's Slant on the Moral
  Climate of Government* (Knowles), 158
Interest rates, on municipal bonds, sewer construction
  and, 32
Internal Revenue Service, 123
International City/County Management Association
  Code of Ethics. *See* ICMA Code of Ethics
Interview process, for chief of police, politicization of,
  15–17
Intuitionist theory, 157
Investments in conflict with official duties, ICMA
  guidelines on, 145

J

Japanese-American relocation program, World War II,
  153
Jefferson, Thomas, 115
Job applicants, convicted sexual molester of children
  among, 4–5
Job rotations, sewer construction project and, 34
Job Training Partnership Act, 130

K

Kant, Immanuel, 154, 157, 160
Killilea, Alfred G., 158
Knowles, Jeffrey, 158
Korean War, 166

L

Ladder 49 (film), 135
Larceny by false pretenses, 124
Lateral arabesque strategy, 75, 76
Law, American Society for Public Administration Code
  of Ethics and respect for, 147
Laws of men, laws of God vs., hiring dilemma and, 5
Leaves of absence, city vehicle use and, 14
Legal interviewing procedures, violation of, 4
Leidlein, James E., 51
Licari, Michael J., 83

Liddy, G. Gordon, 149
Lincoln, Abraham, 19
Little Miss Sunshine (film), 165
Logical irrationality, 157
Longevity pay, 46
Lord of War (film), 165–166
Louisiana Purchase, 115
Loyalty, patronage system and, 100
Lying: Moral Choice in Public and Private Life (Bok),
  154

M

Machiavelli, Niccolo, 158
Malfeasance, 62
Mary case, 79–81
Mary Principle, 79
Mayor, deep involvement of, in police department, 11,
  12
Mayoral election, police force support during, 7–8
McCarthy, Joseph, 165
Media
  allegations by, over police chief's behavior, 16
  child molestation case and, 54
  hostage crisis and, 70
  openness related to police chief interviews and, 15
  taxation matter and, 95, 96, 97
  trustee's arrest and, 86
Mental illness, 41–42
Menzel, Donald C., 154, 158
Merit pay, 28, 46
Mill, John Stuart, 160, 165
Millage referendum, passage of, 97
Minnowbrook groups, 157
Minority populations, police relations and, 12–13
Moore, George Edward, 157
Moore, Michael, 167
Morality, 83
Moral principles, of ethical behavior, 83–90
Morris, Delyte, 151
Munchausen syndrome by proxy, 120–126
Municipal bonds, interest rate dips on, and sewer
  construction grants, 32
Murder, spousal, 39, 42
Murrow, Edward R., 165

N

National Association of Schools of Public Affairs and
  Administration, 155
National Atmospheric and Space Administration,
  153
National Guard, 76
Nazi Holocaust, 153
Negligence suits, against city, 42
Neighborhood grant program, irregularities in, 26–27
New Republic, 167
911 line calls, 39, 42
Nixon, Richard M., 31, 129, 130
No ethic corrupter, 160
Nonfeasance, 62

O

Official duties, ICMA guidelines and investments in conflict with, 145
On the Waterfront (film), 166
Overload problem, sewer construction project and, 34

P

Paine, Tom, 69
Paranoid schizophrenia, 41
Pasquerella, Lynn, 158
Patronage system, 100–103
Paul case, 78–79
Paul Principle, 79
Paul Principle (Armour), 74
Pedophilia, 52, 53, 54
Peripherally inserted central catheter, 118, 121, 126
Personality traits, inappropriate, in police officers, 36–37
Personal life, of building inspector candidate, 65
Personal property, taxes and, 94
Personal relationships, ICMA guidelines on, 145
Peter, Laurence J., 73, 74
Peter case, 74–77
Peter Principle, 75, 79
    corollaries of, 74
Peter Principle, The (Peter and Hull), 73
Philadelphia (film), 166
PICC. *See* Peripherally inserted central catheter
Plagiarism, 23, 45–48
Plato, 35, 157, 160
Player, The (film), 166
Plumbing examination, for building inspectors, 64
Plunkitt, George Washington, 26, 159
Plunkitt of Tammany Hall (Riordon), 159
Police cadet program, C.E.T.A. funding for, 133
Police chief, hiring dilemma for sidewalk project and, 4
Police department, accident-related disabilities and removal from, 57–59
Police infrastructure, development of, in urbanized township, 93
Police officers
    citizen complaints about, 36
    demotions of, 135
    firing of, 133
    prostitutes solicited by, 134
    rivalry among, 69–72
    suspensions of, 37, 132
Police services, ten-mill tax for, 94, 96
Police union, mayor on bargaining team and representation for, 8–9
Political advantages, question of irregularities in community development department and, 25–29
Pork Chop Hill (film), 166
Poverty, 12, 25
Predecessors in office, past illegal tax collections and, 94–95
Preferential treatment, for new vacancies, 34

Presentation of issues, ICMA guidelines on, 143
Private employment, ICMA guidelines and, 145
Producing the output, 73
Professional development, ICMA guidelines on, 143
Professional Ethics (Bayles), 153–154
Professional papers, publication of, 45–46
Professional positions, growing clerical jobs into, 103
Professional respect, ICMA guidelines on, 140–141
Promotions, civil service system for, 40
Property assessment, 106
Property tax levies, 94
Prostitutes, solicitation of, 85, 87, 88, 133–134
Public Administration, Power and Politics in the Fourth Branch of Government (Smith and Licari), 83
Public assistance, 12
Public confidence, ICMA guidelines on, 140
Public Integrity (Dobel), 155–156
Public interest, American Society for Public Administration Code of Ethics and, 146
Public managers, profiles of, 160
Public sector employment, absenteeism and, 46

Q

Quiz Show (film), 167

R

Race, discriminatory hiring practices in police department and, 12
Raises, 81
Ramsey, JonBenet, 165
Rand, Ayn, 164
Rare diseases, 119–120
Reagan, Ronald, 130, 161
Real estate market, downturns in, 131
Real estate taxes, 96
Rebates, tax, 95
Recreation program, hiring for, 79
Reelection campaigns, 26–27, 29
Rehabilitation center, 89–90
Remains of the Day (film), 167
Renovations, city-wide, 20
Replacement cost approach, assessments and, 107, 109
Representation, ICMA guidelines on, 145
Resentments, 74
Residency rules, 40
Resignations
    by chief of police, 14
    from township board, 87
Responsible Administrator, The: An Approach to Ethics for the Administrative Role (Cooper), 155
Resumés, lies on, 20, 21
Retirement
    of building inspector, 62–63
    of incompetent officials, 77
    mandatory age for, elimination of, 75

Retraining, 74, 80
Riordon, William, 159
Rivalries, among police officers, 69–72
Roger and Me (film), 167
Rohr, John A., 159
Role conflicts, ICMA guidelines on, 142
Roosevelt administration, Works Progress
    Administration and, 130
Rotary International, creed of, 93
Rules of Procedure
    for Enforcement of the Code of Ethics, 141
    ICMA, 139
Rumors, 85
Running for office, ICMA guidelines on, 142

S

Salaries, police union, mayor on bargaining team and,
    8–9
Schizophrenia, 41
School district, township bid on land for cemetery and,
    113–115
Schwarzkopf, Norman, 7
Schweitzer, Albert, 117
Self-assessment, ICMA guidelines on, 143
Seniority, 74, 75
Separation pay, child molestation charges and, 55
Septic tanks, 31, 32
Service length, ICMA guidelines on, 141
Sewer construction
    impounding of authorized funds for, 31
    ordinances for, 32
Sewer hotlines, 33, 34
Sexual harassment, police chief and, 16
Sexual molestation, 52, 53, 54
Shattered Glass (film), 167
Sheen, Charlie, 168
Sick leave, 41, 57–58
Sidewalk project
    cancellation of, 5
    C.E.T.A. and hiring process for, 3–4
    explanation of, 1–3
Smith, Kevin B., 83
Socializing, misuse of insider information and,
    70–71
Solicitation of prostitutes, 85, 87, 88, 133–134
Spousal murder, 39, 42
St. Jude Children's Research Hospital, 119, 122,
    123
Stabbing, fatal, 40, 42
State and Local Fiscal Assistance Act, 129
Steinberg, Sheldon S., 159
Stockman, David, 161
Street construction bids, 26
Substance abuse treatment, 89–90
Suicides, by police officers, 133
Super Size Me (film), 168
Supreme Court, 31
Suspensions, of police officers, 37, 132
Svara, James, 160

T

Tammany Hall, 159
Taxes
    annexation and, 111
    assessed values and, 106–107
    discrepancy in application of, 94
    publicizing 27-year-long mistake about, 93–97
    rebates on, 95
Tax ID numbers, 122
Tax millages, raising, for fire and police operations,
    93–94
Taylor, Herbert J., 93
*Teaching Ethics and Values in Public Administration
    Programs: Innovations, Strategies, and Issues*
    (Bowman and Menzel), 154
Teleology, 157
Terminations, 42
    child molestation charges and, 55
    of city manager, 20–21
    of fire fighter, 136, 137
That Championship Season (film), 168
Thompson, William, 31
Thoreau, Henry David, 105
Timmins, William M., 160
Tong, Rosemary, 161
Tornado hits, 35–36, 76
Township purchasing rules, land bids and, 111–115
Traffic accidents, on-duty, 57
Training, investing in, 80
Travel expense billing, 26
Travolta, John, 135, 163
True crime dramas, 117–118
Trustees, ethical examination of, 85–90

U

Unemployment, 33
    C.E.T.A. and, 130–131
    poverty and, 12
Unions
    police officers', 132, 135
    wandering firefighter and, 136, 137
Unmasking Administrative Evil (Adams and Galfour),
    153
Unpaid leaves of absence, 37, 54

V

Value-based ethicist, 160
Valueless or relativistic functionary, 160
Victim complaints, 36
Vietnam War, 157
Vocino, Michael, 158
Voluntary termination, of fire fighter, 137

W

Wall Street (film), 168
Waste, 26

Wastewater treatment plants, federal dollars and
 building of, 130
Water dilemma, 151–152
Watergate scandal, 157
Weapons, reckless discharge of, 41
Web pages, plagiarized passages on, 22–23
West, Jonathan, 161
West Point, motto of, 164

*Whistleblowers, The: Exposing Corruption in
 Government and Industry* (Glazer and Glazer),
 157
Whistle-blowing, 155, 160
Works Progress Administration, 130
World War II, 157, 163
W.P.A. *See* Works Progress Administration